THAT'S NOT HOW YOU WASH A SQUIRREL

ISBN 978-0-9886895-9-6
That's Not How You Wash A Squirrel

www.27bslash6.com

By the same author:

The Internet is a Playground
The *New York Times* bestselling first release by David Thorne featuring articles from 27bslash6 plus over 160 pages of new material.

I'll Go Home Then; It's Warm and Has Chairs
The second collection of all new essays and emails.

Look Evelyn, Duck Dynasty Wiper Blades, We Should Get Them
The third collection of new essays and emails.

That's Not How You Wash a Squirrel
You're holding it.

Wrap It In a Bit of Cheese Like You're Tricking the Dog
The fifth collection of new essays and emails.

Walk It Off, Princess
The sixth collection of new essays and emails.

OFFICE MEMO PRESS

For Seb, Holly & Squirrel.
Every reason.

Scratch 'n Sniff

Reviews

★★★★☆ "There were no instructions but it wasn't difficult to work out. Just make sure you have a friend and a size 11 spanner handy."
Beverly Gardner

★★★★★ "Bought this as a gift for my dad as he lost his hat. He loves it and has received many compliments from elderly women."
Andrew Snell

★★★★★ "It smells terrible but achieved good results with very little scrubbing. My advice is to spray it and run away as quickly as you can."
Richard Morris

★☆☆☆☆ "Not waterproof. I tested it in a bucket of water and it lasted less than ten minutes."
Dave Pease

★★★★☆ "Pros: Took this bad boy camping last week and all of my camp buddies were jealous. Cons: There isn't any way of attaching it to your leg. I tried using Velcro but it fell off when I jumped out of a tree."
Korneel Bullens

Contents

Foreforeword

"Have you finished the book yet?"

"No, Holly."

"How's it going?"

"Fine."

"Can I read it yet?"

"No you can't read it yet. Why would I let you read it if it isn't finished?"

"How close to finished are you then? The deadline was two weeks ago."

"Yes, I realise that. It's not easy you know, not with the dogs barking and having to go shopping and things."

"Perhaps you shouldn't have spent spring and summer building a multi-level amphitheater in the backyard."

"It adds value to the house."

"I'm just saying. If you want me to read it for you before it goes off, that's at least another day or two."

"Yes, I know all this. Telling me I should have finished two weeks ago doesn't make words magically appear on pages. You're meant to be helping."

"I am helping. How many pages do you have left to go?"

"About twenty. Give or take twenty. Give mostly. Plus I have to write a foreword about something."

"What's the foreword going to be about?"

"Who cares. Nobody reads the foreword. I'm only adding

one to flush out the pages. If I knew anybody famous I'd ask them to write it for me. Lots of books have 'foreword by such and such.'"

"You know a couple of famous people. What about the Bloggess or Matthew Inman?"

"Famous people, not famous on the Internet people. Besides, they're both dreadful. All the Bloggess does these days is go on about how depressed she is and Matthew Inman is a bit of a dick."

"How so?"

"He's short and annoying. Plus he looks like the son from *Hardcore Pawn*. Will you write it for me?"

"The foreword? No. I'm not famous."

"It doesn't matter. I'd rather have you write it than Matthew Inman. I read that he once fingered a baby."

"Where did you read that?"

"On Reddit."

"Did you write it?"

"No."

"I can tell when you're lying, you look slightly startled and you flick the tip of your tongue out like a lizard."

"If you write the foreword, it will give me time to finish the rest of the book."

"I don't have time to write the foreword *and* edit the book for you. Some of us work full-time for a living."

"Editing shouldn't be that hard, I've used a spell check."

"It's not the spelling that's the issue. You don't know how to correctly write possessives of plurals or understand that words that end in vowels aren't pluralised with apostrophes."

"Nobody does, Holly. People who do don't read my books, they're too busy reading plays and sonnets."

"If I did agree to write the foreword, and I'm not saying I will, what would I even write it about?"

"About how awesome I am. If *I* write about how awesome I am, I'll just come off as a bit of a dick. Like Matthew Inman. They'll believe it coming from you. All you have to do is say how hilarious I am and what a pleasure it is to have me in your life. Also, something about my writing process and maybe a bit about how brave I am. Remember that time I flicked a snake off the patio furniture with a stick? That's probably worth mentioning."

"Right, well I'm definitely not writing it then."

"Fine, you can write whatever you want. Just don't go off on too many tangents. That's my thing."

"Convolution is a 'thing' most people avoid. So I can write whatever I want?"

"Why? What are you going to write about?"

"About how awesome you are."

"You can't write anything mean. I won't put it in if you just write mean stuff about me."

"I'm not going to be censored before I've typed a single word but I wouldn't just write mean stuff about you. Do you want me to write the foreword or not?"

"No, not if you're just going to write shit about me."

"Good. I've got better things to do."

"See, this is what I mean about not being helpful. Are you going to write it or not?"

"No."

"Just write the fucking foreword, Holly."

"Fine."

"Okay. Thank you. Just don't make it too much better than my stuff. Nobody cares about purplised possessions or who owns all the vowels. Do you think you could have four pages to me by tonight?"

Foreword

By Holly Thorne

You may wonder why I am writing David's foreword instead of someone better equipped. I am too. I haven't even read the book yet. I will however be expected to proofread for content, grammar and syntax at 11pm on a Monday. The fact that I have a meeting at 7am every Tuesday is of no consequence to David; those fortunate enough to be in the writer's circle must accommodate. I will be tired but I will edit my heart out and deliver his marked up manuscript on time. I will also feel bad about myself when one of David's readers emails him asking whether he's ever heard of the 'I before E, except after C' rule.

There are many terms that could be used to describe David's writing process but none as apt as *procrastination*. He has it down to an art form. Procrastinating for nine months on a twelve-month deadline is not something most people would even consider in the real world. Responsibility, pride and self-respect are barriers not everyone can just run around.

David's level 10 ability to procrastinate is not confined to writing of course, he dwells outside the timelines generally accepted by society in all areas. Creative genius cannot be rushed. If you need him to pick you up from work, be on time for a doctor's appointment, or show up before your party is over, ask him to arrive three hours earlier than required. Even then, you will still have a wait as David will have last minute doubts about which of his 140 identical black t-shirts goes best with his hair that day. After changing several times and deciding he should probably also change his watch, he will notice the time, rush from the house, turn on all of the lights as he exits rooms, and leave his wallet, cigarettes and keys resting on a hot stove top. Rather than use the spare Hide-a-Key to retrieve his belongings, David will break a window to get in, grab his stuff, turn on more lights, and leave two hours later with the stove still on.

David does have a stressful job but let's be honest, he's not clearing landmines. Even on my worst days I'm not half the diva that David becomes when he realises he only has six weeks left in which to write two hundred pages. As the months grow cooler and other families snuggle in, World War III breaks out in our household. Unfathomable demands are made and friends, family and pets are committed to walking on eggshells in his presence.

You may assume I'm a glutton for punishment to put up with this shit. You assume right but there's more to it than that. David can be fun, and funny, and caring. Not while he's writing of course, or if he's having a bad hair day, or if the dogs are barking, or if he has to do something before 11am, or `David is very brave, I once saw him flick a snake off the patio furniture with a stick.`

After writing is completed, most authors will rewrite whole paragraphs, even whole chapters, based on editorial feedback. David, however, sees editing as little more than a way to screw up his layout. A glance through any of his books, including this one, will reveal that many of his paragraphs start and end on the same page. Apparently, this is a "design thing." Any suggestion to delete or amend content that causes disruption to this layout is ignored. Grammar and syntax changes are also ignored. Most spelling changes are ignored, all questions regarding made-up words are ignored, and requests to change people's names so we don't get sued are ignored. I'm not sure why I bother.

Somehow, it all comes together. Stacks of boxes containing freshly printed copies of David's latest opus arrive and are signed and mailed off to be lost at dozens of USPS offices, arriving in the letterboxes of pissed off readers several days after Christmas or, for international orders, just before Easter. It's then that David will make grandiose statements like, "Next year, I'll write a few pages each day so I don't have to go through that again."

Perhaps he believes it at the time. After seeing in the new year, David will spend nine months cutting the legs off all of the furniture to "modernize it", move eighteen tons of dirt from one side of the yard to the other, and back again, start several wars with the neighbors, and attempt to build some kind of deck.

As the leaves begin to turn, so will David. In a panic, he will lock himself away in a room with a coffee maker and fifty cartons of Marlboro, pumping out two-hundred odd pages and complaining the whole time about people not being helpful.

Postforeword

"I emailed you the foreword."

"Yes, I'm reading it now."

"Is it alright?"

"Yes, it's fine."

"What's wrong with it?"

"Nothing, I said it's fine."

"I can tell by the way you're saying it that it isn't."

"Well, to be honest, it's not exactly what I was looking for but kind of what I was expecting."

"In what way?"

"There's no mention of the snake and most of it makes me come off as a bit of a fuckwit. I thought, perhaps naively, there might be one kind comment hidden amongst the whining and character assassination but I had a good rummel around and didn't find anything."

"You had a what?"

"A good rummel."

"Do you mean rummage?"

"No, rummel is a word."

"I'm looking it up... there's an Archbishop Rummel but there's no such word as rummel in the dictionary. How do you spell it?"

"Rumle or rummle. It depends on the usage... whether it has verbs."

I'm pretty sure you meant rummage."

Whatever Holly. You're not a Spelling Bee."

"I did write that you can be fun, funny and caring."

"Well yes, but you didn't expand on *how* I'm fun, funny or caring. It's just one small sentence followed by a "but." I suppose there wasn't a lot of room left after the whole 'being a fuckwit' component though."

"I can rewrite it if you want."

"No, it's fine."

"I could have written a lot worse."

"Well that's good to hear. Cheers for that."

"I wrote it with an underlying tone of affection."

"Yes, I'm sure you did."

"I think it comes across."

"I'm sure it does. Perhaps later, if your feeling *really* affectionate, I can pop out and lay down in the driveway for a bit while you back over me with the car."

"You're being a bit dramatic."

"That's what divas do. I doubt you'd be overly impressed if I wrote stuff about you."

"You write stuff about me all the time."

"Nice stuff. I might mix it up a bit this time though. Add some dirt about you. You're hardly perfect either you know."

"What kind of dirt?"

"Just general dirt."

"Give me one example."

"Oh, I could give you twenty examples if I wanted to. Probably thirty."

"You can't actually think of an example, can you?"

"Ha."

"Come on then."

"You have no appreciation for people who risk their lives for you."

"What are you talking about?"

"The snake."

"Oh my god, it was the size of a shoelace and it was six months ago. Thank you for saving me from the snake by flicking it with a long stick. I will be forever in your debt."

"See, that's what I mean. The stick wasn't that long. Probably only three feet or so. I had to get pretty close."

"Greensnakes aren't poisonous. People keep them as pets."

"We're not certain that it was a Greensnake. Besides, you're not an expert on snake poisonability."

"How do you spell that?"

"Poisonability? With two n's I think."

"What else?"

"A p?"

"No, apart from having no appreciation for people risking their lives; what else?"

"You throw things at me."

"Like what?"

"You threw the remote at me just yesterday."

"The batteries were missing. You'd taken them out to use in your mouse and I missed the first ten minutes of *Jeopardy*."

"There you go. *Jeopardy*. That's another thing."

"What about *Jeopardy*?"

"You take it far too seriously. You're not an actual contestant so you don't have to slam down an imaginary buzzer before you answer. It scares the dogs."

"That's hardly a thing."

"Of course it is. And Alex Trebek can't hear you, he's on the television. Even if he could, "that's what I meant" would still be the wrong answer. Yelling at people on the television is another thing. Let's just agree that we both have things and leave it at that."

"No, *Jeopardy* isn't a thing. Neither is the snake."

"Fine. You have no things. You're perfect."

"Thanks."

"No, you're supposed to say something nice back."

"You're hair looks nice today."

"Thanks. I used your conditioner in the little red tube."

"That's foot cream. Would you like me to rewrite the foreword? I don't mind. I'll write that you are brave and funny and make me happy."

"No, it's fine as it is. Nobody reads the foreword anyway. I might delete the bit about my cargo shorts though if it doesn't screw up my layout.

Introduction

by Lori Snell

Hello, I'm Lori.
Well, it was a pleasure
meeting you.
Bye.

The Ride of the Valkyries

My father watched a lot of football and cricket on television when I was young. It's always either football or cricket season in Australia. I followed neither. He was watching the cricket the day my mother took my sister and I to the pool, the day he left. When my offspring Seb was six or seven, my father emailed me and wrote, "I know I wasn't a very good father but I'd like to try to be a good grandfather."

I suppose it was a turning point in his life. The woman he had left my mother for had left him to move in with a security guard named Gary after nearly two decades of marriage. They owned a house together, a large ranch-style home with a tennis court and swimming pool, no kids of their own. There was a large sign on the entry gate that read *For Sale, Price Reduced.*

I stopped the car for a moment, considered reversing back and driving home. I don't know why I'd said, "Okay, that sounds good," when he'd invited us to visit, because it hadn't. It sounded uncomfortable and weird. Not because I had any animosity or 'daddy left me' issues, but because I simply didn't know him.

I glanced over at Seb in the passenger seat, he was playing a game on his phone. I sighed and drove up the long gravel driveway, parking alongside a half-loaded Budget rental truck.

It *was* uncomfortable and weird. Seb had no idea who the old man asking for a hug was. I had no idea who the old man I was shaking hands with was. He was thinner than I remembered, pinker and greyer. The last time I had seen him I was eleven and he must have been in his thirties. He had a moustache back then, a large one the same as his favourite cricketer.

"Did you find the place okay?"
"Yes, we came up the main highway, turned at the Mobil."
"Ah. It's about five minutes quicker if you turn at the Shell before that."
"Really?"
"Yes. Less traffic."
"I'd remember that for next time but as you're moving, there's not much point."
"No, I suppose not."

He had a present for Seb which was a nice gesture. The yellow, red and blue plastic cricket set was a little young for him but it's the thought that counts. Seb was old enough to know to act pleased.

Seb ran about the house exploring while I helped my father load boxes and furniture. There wasn't a lot of it. We didn't talk about anything that had happened over the last twenty-odd years. Which is a good thing I suppose. It was like two strangers chatting in a pub; polite 'sitting at the bar' conversation. There were awkward silences but carrying out boxes gave us an alternative to staring and nodding. He talked about football and cricket but I've never followed either. We talked about cars and the weather instead, and where he was moving to.

It was meant to be a short visit. A test visit to see if there would be further visits. I don't know why I offered to help him move into his new house.

The new house didn't have a tennis court or swimming pool. It was old and musty. The previous occupants must have smoked inside for many years; the walls tinged yellow except where frames had once hung. Floral patterned carpet, which may once have been vibrant reds and greens, was grey and threadbare.

"It certainly has character," I commented, placing a box marked 'pots & pans' on a chipped tile kitchen countertop, "when was it built?"
"1904 according to the real estate agent. Thebarton is an old area. It's not much, I know."
"With a slap of paint it won't be bad, you might even have hardwood floors under the carpet if it's that old."

The carpet was at its worst by the open fireplace. Sparks and a rolling log or two had left burns, some as large as my hand. It was loose where the frayed edge met the stone hearth and we peeled it back to have a look. Beneath the carpet, the foam underlay had crumpled to yellow dust. Beneath that, the dark polished floorboards were lined with overlapping newspaper pages dating back to 1952.

"Wow, they're actually really nice. You wouldn't even need to sand them. Do you want to rip the carpet out now before we bring in any living room furniture?"

"You'd help me do that?"

"Of course. It shouldn't take long and Seb and I didn't have anything planned for the rest of the day."

"I could order pizza delivery later..."

"That works."

"What if the floors are not all as nice as this?"

"They can't be worse than the carpet but we can peel up a few more areas to check if you like. Even if you do need to replace and stain-match a few boards, it'll be cheaper than replacing the carpet and will probably look amazing."

"Alright. I don't have a lot of money after, you know."

"Yes, I'm sure its been an interesting few months."

"A security guard. Can you believe that?"

"Where at?"

"I don't know, she wouldn't tell me. Which corner do you want to start at?"

The trapdoor was in the middle of the living room. It was large, almost five feet across, with heavy cast iron hinges and a round recessed handle. We'd discovered it when we removed the last of the carpet and swept the underlay and newspapers aside. All three of us gripped the heavy round handle and pulled.

"Can I go down?" asked Seb.
"Are you fucking kidding?" I asked, peering below. Wooden steps disappeared into the darkness.
"It must be some kind of cellar," said my father, "I'll grab a flashlight. There's one in the back of the car."
Seb knelt at the edge while we waited for him to return.
"What do you reckon's down there?"
"Spiders."
"There's a switch on the wall a few steps down. I can just see it..." He laid flat and reached down.
"I wouldn't. Something will grab your arm."
Seb pulled his arm up quickly, "like what?"
"I dont know, some kind of demon or something."
"Some kind of demon?"
"Or something. Just wait for him to get back with the flashlight."
Seb reached down and flicked the switch.

A light came on downstairs, illuminating a bare concrete floor and pastel green walls. There were no spiders or demons. I tested the top step, it appeared solid. I did the same with the next. Seb bolted down past me.

The room was large and empty but for a large metal door at one end. Seb rattled the handle, "It's locked."

I've watched enough movies to know that when you come across a hidden cellar and it contains a locked metal door, it's probably locked for a reason and your best bet is to fuck off back up the stairs, close the trapdoor, and nail it down. That wouldn't make for a very interesting story though so the people in the movies always discover a key or amulet that opens the door and then a demon or something tears them to pieces. Sometimes they will mix it up a bit and it's a verse read from an old book or a tune on a music-box that opens the door but the end result is always the same. If there had been a child's doll in the cellar I would have left right there and then.

"The hinges are on this side," said my father, "if we pry the pins out, we'll be able to take it straight off."
"Yes, but should we?"
"What are you talking about?"
"Never mind."
"Dad thinks there's a demon behind it."
"No I don't Seb, stop being stupid."
"Well if there *is* a demon, it's trespassing on my property. I'll grab a flathead screwdriver."
As my father made his way back up the stairs, Seb leaned towards me and whispered, "Do I call him Philip or Grandpa?"
"Whichever you prefer."

"Maybe Grandpa then. I'll see how it goes."

"You'll see how it goes?"

"Yes, I can always swap if it's strange. What do you really reckon is behind the door?"

"Another empty room probably."

"If it's empty, why would the door need to be locked?"

"Shut up Seb."

Philip returned with a screwdriver and pried the pins up and out of the hinges. The heavy door shifted a bit and Seb and I stepped back. I almost asked, "Shouldn't we all have some kind of weapon?" but censored myself in time. Wedging the screwdriver between the door and frame, Philip jimmied them apart a few inches. He shone the flashlight through the gap and then pulled the door fully open. Beyond the doorway, lay a corridor. A long dark corridor.

The beam from the flashlight barely reached the opposite end, two hundred feet or so away, where a metal ladder led up. Philip stepped through the doorway, shining the flashlight over the walls nearby and located a switch. Of the dozen or so lights strung along the corridor, three of them worked and it was more than enough light to make our way. We were silent as we approached the ladder and shone the flashlight up. Above us, was a trapdoor identical to the one in Philips living room.

"We can't just open it," I whispered, "we don't know what's on the other side."

"We didn't know what was on the other side of the metal door either," Philip replied, also whispering.

"Yes, but we're well past the property line of your place now. This is someone else's place. It might be someone else's living room. If I were sitting at home watching television and a trapdoor in the floor suddenly flew open, I'd have a heart attack."

"I could climb up and stick my ear against the trapdoor," suggested Seb, "if I hear a television we can just go back."

"Alright," I agreed, "just be careful."

Seb climbed the ladder until his head was bent against the trapdoor. I held my breath, I could hear Philip breathing deeply through his nose in the silence. Seb knocked loudly on the wood. "Hello?" he yelled.

"What the fuck, Seb?"

"I couldn't hear anything."

"Did I miss the bit of the plan where we all agreed you would bang and yell if you couldn't hear anything?"

"Should I try to lift it?"

"No."

Seb lifted the trapdoor. It was heavy and only moved a few inches before slamming back down.

"Oh my god Seb, climb back down or I'll sell you to the Gypsies."

"No, climb up here and help me. We can't just go back now without knowing what's up here."

"I can."

"Here, hold this," said Philip, handing me the flashlight and pulling himself up the rungs.

"Thanks Grandpa," Seb said, moving to the side to allow Philip room.

"No problem. On three."

On three, the trapdoor flew up, held at its apex for a brief moment, and slammed open with a resounding thud. Dust particles flooded the flashlight beam, diffusing its reach to a few feet beyond the hole.

"What's up there?"

"I don't know," replied Seb, "it's pretty dark. Pass me the flashlight."

I reached up and handed it to his outstretched hand, he swung back up and held the light above his head, flicking it back and forth.

"Oh my god," he said.

"You have to see this," said Philip.

It's annoying when you're watching a program and just at the exciting bit they cut to an advertisement. Unless it's that commercial for the Toyota Tundra with explosions and motor bikes doing jumps to *The Ride of the Valkyries*. Everything is better with *The Ride of the Valkyries*. For those unfamiliar with Wagner's work, it's the tune they play in the movie *Apocalypse Now* when the helicopters fly in to fuck things up. If at all possible, try to imagine *The Ride of the Valkyries* playing through the next few paragraphs as it will make them seem a lot more exciting and might even make up for the disappointing reveal after several pages of buildup.

I climbed the ladder and lifted myself over the edge, standing between Seb and Philip. The warehouse was huge, almost the size of a football field, dark but for a few slivers of light making their way through boarded up windows. Seb panned the light slowly across the wall to our right. A large mural had been painted, badly, of what appeared to be the dance floor from *Saturday Night Fever* fading into a city skyline at night. The city bit was a lot better than the dance floor bit but that's only because it's pretty hard to fuck up black rectangles and yellow dots. Really, they should have just done the whole thing as that. Or maybe just get someone in who knew what they were doing.

Seb shone the light to our left and up, following carpeted stairs to a glassed-in mezzanine. The words 'Snack Bar' were written in Bauhaus Bold behind a wood panelled counter, a poster above a vinyl booth advertised a coke and hotdog combo deal for 99 cents.

"99 cents for a coke and hotdog is pretty good," said Seb.
"Yes, but what is this place?" I asked.

He swung the flashlight to illuminate a carpeted area behind us. Behind a long dusty counter, rows of wooden shelves marked with numbers lay empty. A sign hanging above the shelves, also written in Bauhaus Bold, read 'Skate Hire'.

"It's a rollerskating rink," said Philip.

I did give a heads-up that it wasn't going to be a secret military base with a spaceship hidden under a tarpaulin. I told this story to my friend Geoffrey a few years back and just as I revealed that it was a warehouse - before getting to the rollerskating rink bit - he asked, "Was it full of porn?"

"What?"
"Was the warehouse full of boxes of porn?"
"No. It was a rollerskating rink."
"A what?"
"A rollerskating rink."
"Are you kidding? That's pretty lame. Were there people rollerskating?"
"What? No, it was old abandoned rink. Why would people be rollerskating in the dark?"
"How would I know? I don't rollerskate. Nobody does. I thought it was going to be something exciting."
"And the most exciting thing you could imagine a warehouse containing is boxes of porn?"
"No, but I knew there wasn't going to be a spaceship hidden under a tarpaulin."

Seb and I spent a lot of time at Philip's new house over the next few months. I think he looked forward to our visits. We helped paint the walls and arrange furniture but mainly we went there to skate.

We'd discovered an electrical mains box in an alcove off the skate hire area. Many of the coloured spotlights above the skating rink had blown but there were enough to see by. Three or four faced a large centre mirrorball which splashed the area below with blue and green points of light. The fluorescent lights in the snack bar, bathrooms, and a DJ booth that overlooked the skating rink all worked.

Most of the sound equipment in the DJ booth was still there and operational. Seb tested a microphone and his voice flooded the skating floor. There were no records to play on the turntables but there was an old double-cassette player and a rack of cassettes with handwritten labels like *Sizzlin' Summer Hits 82* and *Sizzlin' Summer Hits 82 tape 2*.

A Coca-Cola branded glass door refrigerator in the snack bar hummed and lit up when we plugged it in. Seb found an apron with the words 'Thebarton Skate Arena' emblazoned across the front. He pretended to serve us from behind the counter when we later ordered pizza to the house and carried it through the corridor to eat in a vinyl booth. Philip pried open an old electronic cash register while we watched in anticipation but there was nothing in it.

There was a small kitchen off the snack bar with a chip-fryer and microwave. A box in one corner was full of skates and Seb and I searched through it for a pair that fit. They were stiff beige leather boots with thin orange plastic wheels that squeaked horribly as we rolled and stumbled awkwardly across the rink to Rod Stewart's *Young Turks* and the theme from *Chariots of Fire*.

Later, we bought rollerblades and became fairly proficient on them - not enough to claim gold if rolling in a circle was an Olympic event, but we could keep our balance and manage to stop. Eventually we were able to skate backwards for a bit and do small jumps. Another box we discovered in a bathroom cubicle was full of skating trophies and we presented them to each other whenever a particularly 'speccy' trick was performed. Philip didn't skate but he seemed to enjoy spending time in the DJ booth.

"And that was the Go-Go's again with their smash hit, *We Got The Beat*. Apparently it's every third song on this cassette. Coming up next, we have a little ditty 'bout two American kids named Jack and Diane..."

We didn't just use the warehouse to skate and listen to bad eighties music. We marked out tennis court lines using duct-tape, raced remote-control cars, and played indoor cricket. Tennis and cricket proved difficult under rotating green and blue points of light so mostly we did just skate and listen to bad eighties music.

Back then, Seb was only with me every second weekend and a few nights between but we spent almost every hour of that time together at the warehouse. For nearly three months the Playstation was left off and toys ignored, our small concrete box in the city became just a place to sleep after getting back from 'Grandpa's House'. We became experts on which brand of oil was best for wheel bearings, which socks were least sweaty. Eighties mix tapes made their way into the car and Seb knew all of the lyrics by heart.

"What does 'never been to me' even mean?"
"I've no idea. It just sounds like she's having a bit of a brag. 'Poor me, I've been undressed by kings and seen some things, mainly in the mediterranean apparently, but I'm not sure who I really am. Please shower me with sympathy while I sip champagne on a boat.'"
"Maybe she has amnesia."
"Maybe. Or maybe she's just a self-absorbed old cow. I mean, if I complained that I've jetted all over the world and rooted queens on boats but I'm not sure who the real David is, I'd be told to get over myself and stop being a prat."
"What do you reckon she saw?"
"Sorry?"
"The bit where she says she's seen some things that a woman ain't meant to see. What do you reckon it was?"
"Secret blueprints I suppose. She doesn't specifically say."
"Blueprints to what?"
"A tank or something."
"I think she's talking about a penis."
"Could be. It's a dreadful song regardless, fast forward it or put on *Tainted Love*."
"Where is it?"
"*Sizzlin' Summer Hits 82* tape 5. Song four, side two."

We thought of the rollerskating rink as ours. That it always would be. We had no idea what the warehouse had been used for prior to it being a skate rink, or why it was connected to Philip's house by an underground corridor, but it didn't matter. It had been boarded up and forgotten, and we had discovered it. It was ours to use however and whenever we wanted. Then it wasn't.

There was no reason for the trapdoor not to open. We had used it just the previous day. It never stuck and there was no lock. Philip and I climbed the ladder and put our shoulders into it together. It wouldn't move. We tried to jimmy it open with a tyre lever and hammer, even walked around the block looking for the boarded-over front entrance. Where we thought it should be were rows of townhouses. They didn't look all that old. Perhaps at the back of one of those townhouses was a courtyard with an old metal door the occupants had never opened. Perhaps it was covered by vines and forgotten. Perhaps we were just looking in the wrong place.

Seb and I rollerbladed at a nearby tennis court a few times after that but it wasn't the same. Joggers stopped to watch us and a tennis player told us off for leaving marks on the surface. Once when we were there, a group of teens threw pinecones at us and when it rained, we couldn't use it all. Eventually we stopped going and when Seb grew out of his rollerblades, we didn't replace them.

We continued to visit Philip for a while but there wasn't much to do at his house. Our visits turned into short visits which became infrequent short visits. Philip watched the football or cricket while we were there. It's always either football or cricket season in Australia. Conversation, about cars and the weather, was kept to commercial breaks. The last time we visited, Philip yelled at Seb for asking if we could try the trapdoor again. It would have meant moving a coffee table and rug again for no reason. Seb had a Playstation and toys at home and I had stuff to do.

It was a quick service. I said a few words about how much Philip loved football and cricket. Seb had chosen the song to play. The box lowered with a clank and whirr as *Centrefold* by the J. Geils Band (*Sizzlin' Summer Hits 82 tape 3*) played at a respectable level in the background.

Philip had never let on that he was sick. Or perhaps he had and I just didn't pick up on it. I vaguely recall him mentioning something about his prostate but I assumed that was something all old men deal with. To be honest, I'd thought he was talking about not being able to maintain an erection and had changed the subject.

There were only a handful of people at the crematorium, I didn't know any of them apart from my sister and I hadn't seen her in several years. She met Seb for the first time and invited us to visit sometime. I told her, "Okay, that sounds good."

The following weekend, while Seb and I were at Philip's house packing his belongings, we tried the trapdoor one last time. It wouldn't open but we thought we heard running and a shout above so maybe someone else had found a way in. Seb tried knocking but there was no answer.

We did visit my sister a few weeks later but there were no secret passageways in her house and neither Seb or I gave a fuck about her origami owls or potplant hangers. Any halfwit with a roll of string and a few sticks can set up an Etsy shop.

Squirrel

There are no squirrels in Australia. Americans seem vaguely surprised by this. At least the ones I speak to. Or, perhaps they simply feign surprise to appear interested in a conversation about squirrels. I feign a series of expressions, including interest, in almost every conversation I have so it's quite possible. It's the polite thing to do. Of course if everyone stopped feigning interest, conversations in general would be a lot shorter and conversations about things you couldn't care less about could be avoided altogether.

"So we took our cat to the vet last week. Turns out the sluggishness was due to her diet. We changed her food to a high protein mix and, almost immediately, she began perking up. When I left this morning, she was sitting in the window meowing at birds outside."
"I have no interest in what you are saying and I wish you would go away."
"Righto then. Bye."

A co-worker recently spent twenty minutes describing to me new curtains she had ordered for her living room due to the previous ones not working overly well with a rug.

To understand the dilemma properly, the rug was also described in detail, along with the sofa fabric that the rug was purchased to match.

I honestly wouldn't care if she lived at the bottom of the ocean with giant squid for curtains. I nodded in an attentive manner but was actually thinking about oxy-acetylene welders and all the things I could make if I owned one. Afterwards, I looked up welders on Amazon but they were far too expensive so I bought a Breville sandwich maker instead.

"Dad, what's for dinner?"
"Toasted sandwiches."
"Again? We had toasted sandwiches yesterday. And the day before that. We've had them every day for the past week."
"They've had different fillings. That's the beauty of toasted sandwiches, the contents are limited only by imagination."
"They've all been cheese."
"Yes, but they've been different brands of cheese. It's not my problem if your palate isn't refined enough to tell the difference between Kraft and Cracker Barrel."
"I'm making toast."

Someone once told me that if you are watching someone weld and you smell toast, it's the back of your eyeballs cooking. If you are making toast while watching someone weld, this information would, of course, be useless.

When I was young, complaining about what you were given for dinner would result in an immediate suspension of television privileges for that night. Which might not seem too harsh but my father's version included a chair next to the television that you had to sit in and watch the rest of the family watching television from. If you tilted forward and turned your head towards the television, he'd aim the remote control towards you and yell, "Pause."

Three 'pauses' and you were 'off' which meant sitting in the chair with a teatowel over your head.

"Wow, you're certainly missing an exciting episode tonight, David. It isn't a holiday resort planet after all, it's a trap set by the Cylons. Starbuck and Apollo are walking straight into it. Perhaps you'll think about that the next time you decide to comment on how lumpy the Gravox® is."

For those not familiar with Gravox®, it's a waterproof brown gravy-flavoured powder to which you add water and stir. When you poke at the resulting lumps, they burst and produce clouds of dust like the slow-motion videos you see of mushrooms shooting spores.

My mother cut her thumb quite badly on the inside edge of a tin of Gravox® one day and required several stitches. She wrote a lengthy letter to the company informing them of the mishap and a few weeks later, a truck delivered two pallets containing thousands of tins of the horrible stuff.

To my father, it was like winning the lottery and practically every evening meal for the next few years was smothered in it. I missed a lot of television during that time.

"Did you watch *Knight Rider* last night?"

"Um... yes."

"Best episode ever. What was your favourite part?"

"The bit where the car talked."

"Kitt talks in every episode."

"I know, right? How awesome would it be to have a talking car?"

"My favourite part was when the bridge was out but Michael pushed the turbo button at the last minute and Kitt flew over it."

"Yeah, that was pretty good. The car should be able to press its own turbo button though."

"What?"

"If the car can talk and do all sorts of other things, it should be able to press its own turbo button when it needs to."

"Then you wouldn't need Michael."

"Apart from pressing the turbo button, the car can drive itself so it doesn't really need Michael anyway. I don't know why Michael doesn't just stretch out in the passenger seat. Or lie down in the back."

"It's his car, he can sit where he wants. Besides, if he was in the back he'd have to reach all the way over to press the turbo button. Did you watch *Diff'rent Strokes*?"

"Um... yes."

"If I was Willis, I'd fuck Kimberley. She's not his real sister. Do you sometimes wish you could jump into a girl's body, like take over her mind, and then go to your house and knock on the door and when you answer say, 'It's me, I'm in this girl's body. Quick, lets have sex?'"

"Um... no."

"No, I don't either. I was just asking if you do."

Interestingly, Dana Plato, the girl who played Kimberly, didn't have much of an acting career after *Diff'rent Strokes*. She posed for *Playboy* and worked at a dry-cleaners before trying her hand at armed robbery. On February 28, 1991, she entered a video store, produced a gun, and demanded money from the register. The clerk called 911 saying, "I've just been robbed by the girl who played Kimberly on *Diff'rent Strokes*." I'm not making this up. She died of a drug overdose a few years later in a Winnebago. The guy who played Willis defeated Vanilla Ice on an episode of *Celebrity Boxing* a few years back so he's doing pretty well for himself. The little black kid and the dad are dead.

Americans are used to the antics of squirrels. They grow up watching them play, chase and feed and I suppose, like most things, familiarity wears wonder into indifference at best. Whenever I point out a squirrel to my partner Holly, she makes a 'hmm' noise with her nose. When I point them out to my friend JM, he also makes the "hmm" noise but follows it up with, "That's a fat one. It'd make a good stew."

I assume he's joking, as he knows I like squirrels, but apparently it's not as funny when you say the same thing about one of his kids.

Some Americans actually hate squirrels. My neighbour Carl, a sad old flappy nippled short man, sits on his back deck with a .22 rifle for hours each day protecting his veggie patch from potential squirrel assaults. It's a tiny veggie patch with only a couple of tomato plants and several aluminium picnic plates hanging from string, but in Carl's mind, he's defending his farm. Each time he manages to kill one of the potential marauders, he raises a fist into the air and makes a loud "Wayhey!" shout of victory. Sometimes he will call his round curly-haired wife outside to impress her with tales of his magnificent marksmanship. Afterwards, Carl strips off, smears the blood of his hunt over his naked body, and masturbates. Okay, that last part isn't true but as I doubt Carl will ever read this, I can write what I want about him. Once, I saw him sucking off a small boy behind his garden shed.

Carl's in his seventies and apparently has a heart condition so hopefully he will be dead soon. If I knew for certain it would cause a heart attack, I'd buy a squirrel costume and an assault rifle, break into his house before sunrise, and stand at the foot of his bed waiting for him to wake up.

It's a shame I don't know people who know people that kill people for money. The people I know only know people who can get kitchen taps at cost or have a used chiminea to sell and it's too late for me to start hanging out with the wrong crowd now. I've seen people in their forties wearing leather jackets and it's just sad. Besides, if I did know people who know people that kill people for money, I'd probably get carried away and people would be dropping like flies.

"David, the client doesn't like the layout. Can you get a revised proof to him by Wednesday?"
"No need."

Several months ago, Carl's war on squirrels didn't bother me as much. I understand that old people require hobbies to fill the hours between eating Fig Newtons and watching *Jeopardy* so I simply countered his smallscale slaughter, as best I could, by scattering fifty-pound bags of pumpkin seeds on our side of the property line every few days to entice the local fauna to stay out of Carl's range.

Then I found Squirrel.

I was mowing the lawn at the time. If he hadn't moved, I might have run right over him.

When I was about eight, my father ran over my pet tortoise Henry with a mower. Henry wasn't killed but lost a fair amount of his shell. My father patched it with duct tape, which was a bit of a piss-poor effort, but Henry seemed happy enough until he was backed over by a car in the driveway a few weeks later.

Perhaps if the shell hadn't been damaged he might have withstood the weight but blame was placed solely on me for "leaving the fucking thing outside all the time." I held a small service for Henry and buried him in an empty Gravox® tin. My father wasn't present at the service because the cricket was on television but he did come outside later to provide constructive criticism on using his hibachi grill plate as a tombstone.

Squirrel was very small with only a thin covering of grey fur. He was far too young to be out of the nest. Assuming he had fallen from a large nearby oak and his mother would be searching for him, I gently picked him up, carried him to a nook between roots at the base of the tree, and covered him with leaves as way of protection from the mid-Spring wind and predators. He was still there when I checked a few hours later.

"Is he dead?" Holly asked.
"I think so," I replied, cradling the tiny still body in my palm, "He's not moving and... no, actually, I can feel his heart beating."
"Maybe he's just cold."
"Maybe," I covered Squirrel with my other hand and blew hot breath between my fingers, "I don't think he's going to live though. Google what you are meant to do when you find a baby squirrel."

"What should we name him?" Holly asked, tapping squirrel queries into her phone.

"Nothing. If we give him a name, it will be sadder when he dies. You know how attached you get to things."

If Holly had her way, we'd have about four-hundred pets. We have two dogs and as far as I'm concerned that's two too many. If they were good dogs, dogs that didn't chew your favourite sunglasses and shit on the rug, I'd be fine with them but that's not the case. One is insane and the other is fat. So fat, that I refuse to be seen in public with her because people point and shake their heads and I can tell they're thinking I'm a bad dog owner and probably force-feeding the poor thing. Laika looks like a barrel with thin sticks sticking out the bottom and the size of her body makes her head look tiny. I'll try drawing her so you can get a better idea...

You may be thinking, 'Oh David, don't be silly, obviously you've exaggerated the size of Laika's body for comedic purposes', but it's actually an incredibly accurate likeness and I'm considering entering it in this year's Archibold Prize.

Once, while chasing a thrown stick, she tripped and rolled down a hill. It was like the scene in that movie where Han Solo finds a gold monkey in a cave. If she was human, her name would be Louise and her hobbies would include blocking exits, cake, and writing formal complaints. Our other dog, a dalmatian named Banksy, thinks he's an interior decorator and highly objects to decorative pillows being placed on anything in the house. At one point, I was picking decorative pillows off the floor and placing them back on sofas twenty or more times per day, now we just leave them where they are and walk around them. Also, if you look at Banksy, he becomes extremely upset so eye contact is avoided at all times. Looking at him while he's rearranging the living room creates a meltdown and your only option at that point is to curl into a ball and protect your head. If he was human, his name would be Kyle or Hunter and he'd be on ADD medication. We'd receive regular letters from his teacher regarding behavioural issues and later, he'd join the army.

If we hadn't given the dogs names, it would be a lot easier on Holly should I ever decide to drive them out into the woods and leave them there. They'd be fine. Banksy would probably join a wolf pack and Laika could live on her fat reserves for at least six months.

It could be worse of course, they could be cats. Or electric eels. We had a third dog, because we're idiots, but that one died earlier this year. It was on about $800 worth of medicine a week and because I complained a lot about the expense, when the dog finally said, "fuck this" and keeled over, Holly implied a few things and declared that she was getting an autopsy done, which was pretty rude.

A coworker recently accused me of being a sociopath because I "lack the emotional inner worlds that most people have and am therefore incapable of understanding the emotional worlds of other people."

Which isn't true. It's possible to understand, without caring, that someone may be upset when they thought their cat was getting better but then found it dead on the kitchen floor when they got home that night. I mean, if it had been their child I'd have no problem with them taking three days compassion leave and really, there is very little difference between the terms, "Be strong and carry on," and "Walk it off, Princess."

Sobbing behind a locked door won't bring the cat back and other people need to use the photocopier. I took one of those 'Are you a sociopath?' quizzes online that afternoon and it said I wasn't. It wasn't hard to work out where each question was heading though.

I've recreated the test on the next page just in case you'd like to take it yourself.

Are You a Sociopath?

Answer these 6 questions to find out!

1. You've just hurt someone's feelings. How do you feel?
A. Guilty   **B.** Good   **C.** I don't care

2. An old lady leaves a bag full of money on a bench. What do you do?
A. Tell the old lady   **B.** Take the money   **C.** Ignore it

3. You're having a conversation. What do you do?
A. Nod and smile   **B.** Hold eye contact without blinking
C. Ignore them

4. An obese person sits next to you during a flight. What do you do?
A. Smile and say hello   **B.** Tell them to move   **C.** Move

5. You're having an argument with someone who presents a fact that proves you wrong. What do you do?
A. Concede your error   **B.** Become Angry
C. Change the topic

6. You've witnessed a terrible car accident involving a death. How does that make you feel?
A. Upset   **B.** Entertained   **C.** Bored

Answers:
Mostly A: You're not a sociopath.
Mostly B and/or C: You may be a sociopath.

This is probably the test that professional psychiatrists and psychologists use and seems legit. In question 3 though, answering A wouldn't work if the conversation is about finding a dead cat on the kitchen floor and question 4 is a bit dodgy regardless of the answer. I fully support discrimination against fat people but if one sat next to me on a plane I wouldn't move, ask them to move, *or* talk to them. I'd just be quietly annoyed the whole flight and try to breath through my mouth.

Squirrel made it through the night. As per online instructions, we'd placed him in a box with a fluffy towel and hot water bottle. After an hour or so, he opened his eyes and was alert enough to be fed whipping cream through an improvised syringe constructed from a Bic® pen. In the morning, we found him on top of the television making baby pig noises.

I carried Squirrel outside and placed him on a branch of the large oak. He climbed a few feet, seemed to think about it, then ran back down and jumped onto my shoulder. I went inside and ordered about three-hundred dollars worth of baby squirrel formula, syringes, and toys from Amazon.

Over the next few weeks, I became an expert on squirrel requirements and behaviour. When he wasn't feeding or playing, Squirrel lived on my shoulder and slept in my hoodie pockets.

When I was young, I read a story about a fox and a prince. I don't recall how it went exactly but basically a prince ventures out into the forest and sees a fox. He asks the fox if he can pat him and the fox declines. The prince demands the fox let him pat him because he's the prince and the fox explains that's not how it works; in order to trust the prince, the prince must come back each day and sit in the same spot. Oh, I forgot to mention the fox can talk and the prince is lonely because his dad, the king, doesn't spend any time with him. Also, I think the fox was wary because the king hunted foxes. The prince does what the fox says and each day, the fox takes a step closer to him. Either the fox took really small steps or the initial distance between the two was fairly large because this went on for a while. Summer passed, leaves fell, and it began to snow. One day the prince didn't come home so the king went searching for him and found him sitting in a clearing in the forest, frozen to death, with the fox curled in his arms.

I get that it's an analogy of some kind but the story annoyed me at the time as it was never clear on whether the fox was also frozen or fine. If he was also frozen, the time the prince spent sitting might have been better spent collecting firewood or building a small shelter and if the fox was fine, it was all a bit of a dick move. Also, did the king declare, "I will never hunt foxes again," or was he pissed and decide to step up the whole hunting foxes thing a notch? Perhaps my neighbor Carl found his son frozen holding a squirrel. Then fingered him.

There was no sitting, fairy-steps, or freezing to death required to develop trust between Squirrel and I, it was immediate and easy. He showered with me, worked on the laptop with me, and watched television with me. His favourite shows were *Tosh.O*, *The Walking Dead*, and everything on Velocity except *Wheeler Dealers*. You're not Punky Brewster, Edd. Buy a jacket. I learned Squirrel's grunts, squeals and pucker noises and we had lengthy conversations about pumpkin seeds and girl squirrels. We built a squirrel house together using online plans of Frank Loyd Wright's *Falling Water* and when he had outside play time on the lawn or in the large oak, I watched for hawks.

"What are you doing?"

"Giving Squirrel a bath."

"Where did you get the little bathtub?"

"Online. It was only $49.99"

"How much was it really?"

"$49.99"

"You're flicking your tongue out so I can tell you're lying."

"Fine, it was $84.99"

"Why do you lie when I ask you how much you paid for things?"

"I don't know, to protect myself I suppose."

"From what?"

"Admonishment. For spending $84.99 on a little bathtub. It looked a lot better in the photos. It was meant to come with a little rack for soaps and sponges that goes across but it wasn't in the box."

"Can I wash him?"

"Really?"

"Yes, why? Don't you think I'm capable?

"I'm sure you are, it's just that he likes to be washed a certain way."

"Are you joking?"

No, he doesn't like it when you wash his feet so I just let him wade and you have to squeeze out his sponge a bit before wiping his face otherwise he carries on about it and when you wash his tail you can't..."

"Oh my god, just let me wash him."

"Fine..."

"...What?"

"I didn't say anything, Holly."

"'Standing there watching me is the same thing. I can feel you thinking I'm doing something wrong."

"I can't help your imagination. Don't let soap get in his eyes."

"I'm not going to get soap in his eyes."

There's a big drip right next to his left eye. He'll go blind if he gets soap in his eyes and then he won't be able to fend for himself."

"Fend for himself? He's receiving a sponge bath in a miniature Victorian claw-foot tub."

"He seems to like it though."

"Yes, see? Washing a squirrel isn't rocket science."

"I meant the tub, not the way you're washing him."

"What's in the other box?"

"Oh, that? Just stuff."

"What stuff?"

"A little dining table and chairs."

Over the next few months, Squirrel grew bigger and the weather grew warmer. I moved his house outside to our covered porch and constructed a system of walkways from our deck to the large oak, allowing him to come and go as he pleased. Other squirrels lived in the oak, perhaps his brothers and sisters. He'd interact with them occasionally but it wasn't a world he seemed to understand or crave and he always headed home after short visits. At this point, his house had two extensions, solar powered heating, and a pantry off the main corridor stocked with corn, seeds and pizza crusts. His main bedroom, with ample room for two should he meet a girl squirrel and invite her over, featured grasscloth wallpaper, soft lighting, and regularly changed linen. The guest room wasn't used much so became a kind of catch-all room for the treadmill and various sporting equipment.

"His house is nicer than ours," Holly commented, "If I could shrink down to his size, I'd move in."

"That wouldn't work. You'd have to stay in the guest room and it's a bit messy at the moment. Besides, I don't know how Squirrel would feel about having a house guest. He likes his space."

"You do realise that you've gone a bit insane with the whole thing, don't you? I mean, I understand that you love him but..."

"I don't *love* him. He's just a squirrel and that would be

stupid. Wanting him to be happy and safe isn't love, I simply have a call of duty."

"Do you mean *duty of care*?"

"It's the same thing."

"Not really. You love him more than you love the dogs."

"Well that's a given."

"I think you love the squirrel more than you love me."

"Now you're just being silly. I have a responsibility to protect Squirrel, he's small and innocent while you're..."

"Yes?"

"Capable of looking after yourself. Do you want to come for a drive to the hardware store?"

"What for?"

"I need to buy tiles for his pool."

"You're building a swimming pool for the squirrel?"

"It's more of a splash pool. I'm not adding a diving board or anything."

I didn't end up building the splash pool that day. When Holly and I returned from the hardware store, Squirrel wasn't in his house. I stood under the large oak puckering, squealing and grunting but he didn't reply. Hours went by. He'd never stayed out for this length of time. What if he had ventured too far and got lost? What if a hawk had taken him? What if he was injured somewhere, possibly after bravely fighting off a hawk, and calling out for me weakly? We play-fought all the time and he was pretty good at it... he wouldn't just let himself be carried off and ripped apart... I couldn't stand the thought of that...

At the back of Carl's property, adjoining ours, is a small ravine where Carl throws his lawn clippings, fallen branches and other assorted rubbish. I found Squirrel there. He was easily identifiable from the other dead squirrels. Even with his fur matted with blood from the .22 caliber bullet hole, I knew every marking.

Many years ago, when I was studying design, I shared a rental house with a guy named Daniel. We had a third housemate named Todd but he was rarely seen as he worked nightshift as a chicken boner for the local Ingham chicken processing factory. Todd contributed little in the way of cleaning or groceries but a constant supply of free chicken made up for giblet covered overalls in the bathroom and taking food that wasn't his.

"He's eaten all the chips. Even the salt and vinegar ones. And look at this tub of margarine, I only bought that yesterday. It's like he scoops it out by the handful."
"How are we for chicken?"
"There's about... seventy packets of breast and... forty packets of nuggets. We're getting low on schnitzels though. I might leave him a note."

Daniel and I were doing the same course, four years of study towards a bachelor of visual communication, at an Adelaide university. Both of us lived and breathed design at that time but Daniel was a *lot* better. Some people have an eye for design, Daniel felt it. The corporate identities he produced were world standard, his interface designs simplistically beautiful, and his grids a perfect balance of form, function and negative space. Projects that took me weeks to complete, took him days. I wasn't jealous of his abilities, I fed off his enthusiasm and enjoyed his company. Work I submitted was better because of his influence.

Late in third-year, I overheard a private conversation between Daniel and one of our lecturers in which he was told, "At this point, I'm learning more from you than you are from me." By mid-fourth year, several highly respected international branding agencies had offered him positions upon completion of his studies.

Daniel also had a girlfriend named Rebecca. She was studying art at a different school. You could tell when Rebecca stayed over as the house stank of patchouli. All art students wear patchouli as it's a known fact that the oil is a magic repellant against criticism and having to get a real job. She was kind of annoying in the way that all art students are kind of annoying; dirty and poor. We had one of her paintings on the wall of our living area titled *Self Portrait 28*.

"It's pretty big," I commented when it was first hung.
"A large statement deserves a large canvas," Rebecca explained.
"So, it's you on a horse?"
"It's an expression of joy, movement, and freedom."
"Shouldn't the horse be in motion then? It's just standing

there looking anything but joyful. Is it crying?"

"They're tears of happiness. And the horse *is* in motion."

"Its legs would be bent if it was in motion. They're sticking straight down."

"It's jumping."

"Straight up?"

"It's easy to criticise."

"Correct."

"An inability to interpret art says a lot more about the viewer than the artist. It's not my job to explain."

"Granted. You weren't overly helpful with the title though, you should have called it *Rebecca's Happy Hover Horse*."

Daniel and I often drove to classes together and, one afternoon following a cancelled seminar, drove home together early. As we entered the hallway, we heard the sound of people having sex from behind Todd's closed bedroom door and chuckled quietly.

"Todd's getting lucky," Daniel whispered as we made our way into the kitchen, "Good for him. It sounds like she goes off." He made coffee and we sat at the kitchen table flicking through copies of *Desktop* and *MacUser* magazines.

"Does it reek like a mouldy basement in here?" I asked.

The noise from Todd's room stopped. There was a thump and the bedroom door opened.

"Where are you going?" we heard Todd ask.

"I need to take a piss," replied Rebecca, "I'll be right back..."

She froze, naked in the hallway, staring at Daniel and I.

"Grab the tub of margarine on your way back," yelled Todd, "I want to fuck you in the bum. And see if Daniel has bought any more chips."

Daniel didn't finish the university course. Instead, he ran over Todd with his car and set fire to Rebecca's parents house. Apparently he'd only intended to set her car ablaze but the flames travelled up a fence and into the roof of an attached garage containing canvas and paint supplies. The occupants escaped but their cat and two dogs burnt to death.

Todd spent six months in hospital with a crushed pelvis and Daniel spent six years of a ten year sentence in jail. Daniel sent me a friend request on Facebook a while back and I viewed his profile. He lives in a small suburb of Adelaide with his wife and four kids and works for a distribution company as a forklift driver.

I wanted to run Carl over with my car. I wanted to torch his house. I wanted to salt his veggie patch and take out an ad in the local classifieds offering cheap mowing services with his number listed. Carl was my chicken boner and dirty art student girlfriend. Perhaps it wasn't the best example but I'm not going to go back and rewrite three whole pages. I could have written about the time my sister drew a voice bubble on my Ace Frehley poster saying, "I'm gay" and my retaliatory stabbing of her waterbed with a steak knife but having to spend your pocket money on a rubber repair kit is hardly the same as doing hard time. I did once spend three days in jail but that was just for unpaid parking fines. I didn't get bummed or shanked so it's hardly a tale of revenge and repercussion. It's more a tale of playing chess with an old guy named Roger.

Not that I haven't encountered my fair share of chicken boners and dirty art students over the years. I've known betrayal and deceit and each has born its own fantasies of retaliation. In my mind, I have extracted revenge of biblical proportions dozens of times. The kind of revenge where the body count rises as smoke slowly clears. The kind of revenge where I join a mountain-based monastery for several years and learn martial arts. The kind of revenge where there are no repercussions, just a thumping soundtrack that drops the beat at the exact moment I kick down the door holding a GE M61 Minigun.

I had to Google, *'What's that gun that goes wrrrrr in the movie Predator?'* to find out what it's called. Apparently the GE stands for General Electric, which is interesting. I own lightbulbs made by the same company.

Holding Squirrel, I marched up the path between our house and Carl's. I have no idea what my intent was. I didn't drive or take a lighter. I knocked loudly on the front door and waited. There was no answer. The top section of the door contained glass panels, I cupped my free hand over the glass and peered into the small living and dining area. Apart from a partly completed jigsaw puzzle of an autumnal scene on the dining table, it was the exact opposite of a Pottery Barn catalogue photoshoot. There were only two dining chairs and the worn linoleum flooring was lifting in places. The walls, carpet, and velour sofa were all the same shade of beige, broken only by yellowing doilies and a faded print of Gogh's Sunflowers. A vintage wooden television unit sat in the corner with an empty vase and ceramic horse on top. My grandparents had the same exact ceramic horse in their guest room, its head twists off and there's cologne inside.

There were no bookcases stacked with favourite novels, no knickknacks from places visited, no photos. A tangible nothingness, a not mattering, radiated outwards beyond the glass and I stepped back to avoid its touch.

Holly rubbed the fur on Squirrel's neck as I dug a hole. We buried him at the foot of the large oak and smoothed the dirt over. It was as if he had never existed, never mattered, but he did. For a brief moment, he was the most important thing in the world. He was funny, gentle, stupid and loved.

The next day, I drilled anchor points between branches in the oak tree, about six feet from the ground, and secured Squirrel's house there. I keep his pantry stocked and squirrels visit regularly. Sometimes there are three or four at a time. They like pumpkin seeds the best but I add peanuts and corn for variety. I ended up finishing the pool. Birds tend to use it more than squirrels but I've seen squirrels drink from it occasionally and they like sitting on the diving board.

Yesterday, when I lifted the roof to top up the pantry, I noticed something move beneath the linen in Squirrel's bedroom. I peeled back a corner and discovered four baby squirrels. They were pink and bald, no larger than my thumb. I rubbed one gently on the head before closing the lid and Windexing the solar panel. None of them have names because I don't want Holly to get too attached.

I watched Carl wash his Ford Fiesta from our kitchen window this morning. He washes and shines it thoroughly before he takes it out for a drive and washes and shines it thoroughly before putting it back in his garage. It fills a few empty hours. I have no idea where he drives to. Perhaps he just drives around. He's never out long. Except Sunday mornings. Today, his round curly-haired wife helped by vacuuming the floor mats while he Pledged the hub caps. I couldn't hear them from my vantage point so I have no idea what the ensuing argument was about but I saw him raise a hand and saw her flinch away. Perhaps she missed a spot. Perhaps he was just in a bad mood after discovering his tomato plants had disappeared during the night. The gardening stakes were snapped in half and a wheelbarrow was on its side so it was probably a bear or something.

Tomotes

From: Carl Mishler

Date: Tuesday 14 July 2015 2.11pm

To: Ben and Shirley Goertz, Carol McKensie, Joe McKensie, David Thorne, Sue Knowles, Rob Ellis, Janice Roberts

Subject: Trespassing

Dear Residents of the Forest Hill Subdivision,

I dont have the Beasleys email because its not on the subdivision contact list but Ill put a copy of this in their mailbox.

As some of you already know there someone trespassed on our property have been two instances of trespass on our property in the last 5 days. On thursday night someone stole tomato vines and vandalized property so I planted new vines on Sunday and some time that night they were also stolen.

I have my suspicions about whoes responsible and I passed those suspicions on to the local police yesterday. I also bought a trail camera today and its set up to cover the area.

When we establish the person responsible and its only a matter of when not if I'll be pressing charges.

Id also reccomend that the person whoes responsible remember that I have a legal right to protect my property and I own a firearm.

Carl Mishler

....

From: David Thorne
Date: Tuesday 14 July 2015 2.41pm
To: Carl Mishler
CC: Ben and Shirley Goertz, Carol McKensie, Joe McKensie, Sue Knowles, Rob Ellis, Janice Roberts
Subject: Re: Trespassing

Dear Carl,

It was probably a bear or something.

Regards, David

From: Carl Mishler
Date: Tuesday 14 July 2015 3.02pm
To: David Thorne
CC: Ben and Shirley Goertz, Carol McKensie, Joe McKensie, Sue Knowles, Rob Ellis, Janice Roberts
Subject: Re: Re: Trespassing

It wasnt a bear I know what bear tracks look like and a bear wouldnt take the vines completely out of the ground. This is a quiet community and we dont put up with this kind of BS around here.

I know exactly whoes responsible and its only a matter of time before charges are laid.

Carl Mishler

....

From: David Thorne
Date: Tuesday 14 July 2015 3.12pm
To: Carl Mishler
CC: Ben and Shirley Goertz, Carol McKensie, Joe McKensie, Sue Knowles, Rob Ellis, Janice Roberts
Subject: Re: Re: Re: Trespassing

Was it Janice? I bet it was. She looks a bit shifty. Did you notice any walking-frame indentions?

From: Janice Roberts
Date: Tuesday 14 July 2015 4.24pm
To: Carl Mishler, David Thorne, Ben and Shirley Goertz, Carol McKensie, Joe McKensie, Sue Knowles, Rob Ellis
Subject: Re: Re: Re: Re: Trespassing

It wasn't me.

From: Janice Roberts
Date: Tuesday 14 July 2015 4.26pm
To: Carl Mishler, David Thorne, Ben and Shirley Goertz, Carol McKensie, Joe McKensie, Sue Knowles, Rob Ellis
Subject: Re: Re: Re: Re: Trespassing

Why would I steal tomotes?

From: Janice Roberts
Date: Tuesday 14 July 2015 4.28pm
To: Carl Mishler, David Thorne, Ben and Shirley Goertz, Carol McKensie, Joe McKensie, Sue Knowles, Rob Ellis
Subject: Re: Re: Re: Re: Tresspassing

We have our own.

From: David Thorne
Date: Tuesday 14 July 2015 4.47pm
To: Carl Mishler, Janice Roberts
CC: Ben and Shirley Goertz, Carol McKensie, Joe McKensie, Sue Knowles, Rob Ellis
Subject: Re: Re: Re: Re: Re: Tresspassing

Carl,

Do you think you could tell your tomatoes from Janice's tomotes in a line-up?

Janice, do you mind if Carl and I come over to inspect your patch? What time would suit? Carl's an early riser but he won't be able to make it before noon if he decides to drive. You don't have to provide lunch or anything.

Unless you want to.

While I've little doubt the FBI will be stepping in at any moment to take over the investigation, I'm sure they'd be thankful for any evidence we can procure in the meantime to help with their case against Janice.

Regards, David

From: Carl Mishler
Date: Wednesday 15 July 2015 9.20am
To: Janice Roberts
CC: Ben and Shirley Goertz, Carol McKensie, Joe McKensie, David Thorne, Sue Knowles, Rob Ellis
Subject: Re: Re: Re: Re: Re: Tresspassing

I know it wasnt you Janice I know exactly who it was. Im planting more vines today and if there stolen again Ill have more than enough evidence to press charges.

Carl Mishler

....

From: Carl Mishler
Date: Thursday 16 July 2015 3.36pm
To: Ben and Shirley Goertz, Carol McKensie, Joe McKensie, David Thorne, Sue Knowles, Rob Ellis, Janice Roberts
Subject: Neighborhood watch

Dear Residents of the Forest Hill Subdivision,

Yesterday I planted 4 tomato vines to replace the ones that were stolen last night they were stolen again A trail camera that cost $79.99 was stolen as well and our wheelbarrow was found in Janices front yard. I reported the theft and an officer spoke to the person I believe is responsible I wont name any names you know who you are.

He also reccomended setting up a neighborhood watch among residents to report suspicious activity. If youd be interested in participating let me know by email or call me on (540) 740 8354.

Carl Mishler

....

From: David Thorne
Date: Thursday 16 July 2015 3.59pm
To: Carl Mishler
CC: Ben and Shirley Goertz, Carol McKensie, Joe McKensie, Sue Knowles, Rob Ellis, Janice Roberts
Subject: Re: Neighborhood watch

Hello Carl,

An officer also spoke to me, I told him it was probably a bear or something.

Regardless, I'd be more than happy to participate in a neighbourhood watch program. I would, however, prefer the term 'vigilante team' as 'neighborhood watch' makes it sound like it's just going to be a bunch of sad old farts gossiping. It's your call though, I'm not the boss of our vigilante team.

I took it upon myself to whip up a quick logo. I can have t-shirts made up before our first meeting if everyone sends me their sizes. I'm guessing you're a child's medium?

The shirts are $25 each but if everyone could put in an extra $10 for my trouble it would be appreciated.

Regards, David

....

From: Carl Mishler
Date: Thursday 16 July 2015 4.17pm
To: David Thorne
CC: Ben and Shirley Goertz, Carol McKensie, Joe McKensie, Sue Knowles, Rob Ellis, Janice Roberts
Subject: Re: Re: Neighborhood watch

That wont be neccesary because your not invited. Ive been polite to you since you moved here but your definitely not welcome in my house.

Carl Mishler

From: David Thorne
Date: Thursday 16 July 2015 4.20pm
To: Carl Mishler
CC: Ben and Shirley Goertz, Carol McKensie, Joe McKensie, Sue Knowles, Rob Ellis, Janice Roberts
Subject: Re: Re: Re: Neighborhood watch

Because I'm black?

....

From: Carl Mishler
Date: Thursday 16 July 2015 4.31pm
To: David Thorne
CC: Ben and Shirley Goertz, Carol McKensie, Joe McKensie, Sue Knowles, Rob Ellis, Janice Roberts
Subject: Re: Re: Re: Re: Neighborhood watch

Your not black.

From: Rob Ellis
Date: Thursday 16 July 2015 4.42pm
To: Carl Mishler, David Thorne
CC: Ben and Shirley Goertz, Carol McKensie, Joe McKensie, Sue Knowles, Janice Roberts
Subject: Re: Re: Re: Re: Re: Neighborhood watch

My phone gives me a notification every time you send an email. Everyone's forwarding the emails to everyone else and my email address is in the list. I've received 20 notifications in the last hour. I haven't got time to go to team meetings and nobody gives a fuck about missing tomatoes.

Please take me off this email list.

Rob

....

From: Rob Ellis
Date: Thursday 16 July 2015 4.46pm
To: Carl Mishler, David Thorne, Ben and Shirley Goertz, Carol McKensie, Joe McKensie, Sue Knowles, Janice Roberts
Subject: Re: Re: Re: Re: Re: Neighborhood watch

Sorry for the language. I didn't mean to include everyone in that email.

Rob

From: Carl Mishler
Date: Thursday 16 July 2015 5.09pm
To: Rob Ellis
CC: Ben and Shirley Goertz, Carol McKensie, Joe McKensie, David Thorne, Sue Knowles, Janice Roberts
Subject: Re: Re: Re: Re: Re: Re: Neighborhood watch

It's not a team Rob just communication between residents for everybodies benefit and saftey. Ill make a neighborhood watch mailing list that everybody will be included on and send updates once or twice a week. Wed only meet at my house once a month for about 30 minutes.

Carl Mishler

....

From: David Thorne
Date: Thursday 16 July 2015 5.37pm
To: Rob Ellis
CC: Ben and Shirley Goertz, Carol McKensie, Joe McKensie, Carl Mishler, Sue Knowles, Janice Roberts
Subject: Re: Re: Re: Re: Re: Re: Neighborhood watch

Hello Rob,

Would you be interested in starting our own vigilante team? This way we could organise meetings around your schedule. Every second Wednesday at Janice's house around dinner time works for me but I'm flexible.

As Carl's group appears to add little to the system already in place - apart from the threat of even more emails devoid of grammar, punctuation, correct spelling or point - I propose our group's rules consist only of regularly not attending meetings and keeping all communication to a wave as we drive past. It doesn't have to be a big wave, the one where you raise a few fingers off the steering wheel and nod is fine. Or one finger for Carl. With or without the nod.

The main benefit of our group would be not having to visit Carl's tiny house of sadness. I looked though his window recently and it was like having two syringes of pure beige injected directly into my corneas. I actually staggered home and had to flick through Pantone colour swatches to stop shaking. Carl wasn't home at the time - unless he was wearing his Sunday morning beige suit and I simply didn't notice him. Given the choice between thirty minutes in Carl's house or thirty hours in a cardboard box, I'd pick the less beige and roomier option. Any meeting at Carl's house involving more than two people will have to be held standing in a tight circle and thirty minutes is far too long to have to stare at Carl's head that close. It's like a shaved pug that's been dragged behind a car for several miles then left in the sun.

The one and only benefit I can see to attending Carl's neighborhood watch meetings is that he's probably less likely to beat his wife with witnesses present.

Regards, David

From: Rob Ellis
Date: Thursday 16 July 2015 6.01pm
To: David Thorne
CC: Ben and Shirley Goertz, Carol McKensie, Joe McKensie, Carl Mishler, Sue Knowles, Janice Roberts
Subject: Re: Re: Re: Re: Re: Re: Re: Neighborhood watch

Sounds good to me.

....

From: Carl Mishler
Date: Thursday 16 July 2015 6.13pm
To: David Thorne
CC: Ben and Shirley Goertz, Carol McKensie, Joe McKensie, Sue Knowles, Rob Ellis, Janice Roberts
Subject: Re: Re: Re: Re: Re: Re: Re: Neighborhood watch

I'm blocking your email and removing you and Rob from my mailing list. We'll let the man deal with theft and defamation charges.

Carl Mishler

From: Ben and Shirley Goertz
Date: Thursday 16 July 2015 6.30pm
To: Carl Mishler
CC: Carol McKensie, Joe McKensie, Sue Knowles, Rob Ellis, David Thorne, Janice Roberts
Subject: Re: Re: Re: Re: Re: Re: Re: Re: Neighborhood watch

Hello Carl, can you remove us from your list too please?

Thank you, Ben and Shirley

....

From: Carol McKensie
Date: Thursday 16 July 2015 7.04pm
To: Carl Mishler
CC: Ben and Shirley Goertz, Joe McKensie, Sue Knowles, Rob Ellis, David Thorne, Janice Roberts
Subject: Re: Re: Re: Re: Re: Re: Re: Re: Neighborhood watch

Hi Carl,

Kate moved over a year ago and I don't think that email works anymore. Its her old work one.

Would you mind also taking mine and Joe's off of the mailing list?

We get a lot of spam and we're with Hughesnet so we can only check our email when it's sunny.

Carol

....

From: Janice Roberts
Date: Friday 17 July 2015 10.23am
To: Carl Mishler, David Thorne, Ben and Shirley Goertz, Carol McKensie, Joe McKensie, Sue Knowles, Rob Ellis
Subject: Re: Re: Re: Re: Re: Re: Re: Neighborhood watch

I have my kaffeeklatsch on wednesdays.

Encarta 95

It's an easy joke to declare, "Lol, old people and computers" and then shrug and shake your head while giving a helpless knowing smile as if to say 'whatcha gonna do?' Maybe make a noise with your nose by blowing out quick. You could also hold your arms out with your palms up but that's pushing the whole thing a bit.

Holly and I purchased her parents a laptop for their anniversary. They owned a computer but it had passed its use-by date somewhere around the turn of the century. I'm not exaggerating, it had a yellowed sticker on it stating it was Y2K ready. Somehow it still ran. It didn't need to do much and Tom and Marie were happy to "go and watch a bit of TV while it reboots." We should have left good enough alone.

"We've already got a computer."
"I know Tom, but this one is a lot newer. There have been a few advances since manufacturers switched over from vacuum-tube technology."
"Ours still works. I used it last week."
"What for?"
"To see if it still works."
"Yes, but what did you use it for?
"Nothing. I just turned it back off. Never had a problem with it."

We spent an hour or so showing them how to use their new Chromebook. Tom wasn't overly interested and Marie commented on how shiny it was several times and seemed more concerned about what to use to clean it than the features it offered. The absence of a CD drive caused Tom some concern as they owned a copy of Encarta 95.

"When was the last time you used the Encarta 95 disks?"
"Doesn't matter. We own them."

Approximately two hours after Tom and Marie packed the laptop carefully back in its box and left for home, the phone calls began. Holly fended off the first couple of calls but quickly switched to saying, "Hang on, I'll pass you to David" as if on autopilot. The following twelve transcripts are from that evening's calls alone:

Marie, 5.20pm

"Tom had it on his lap and his knees got hot so we turned it off and packed it back in the box. Do you still have the receipt?"

Marie, 5.42pm

"Tom opened the program that records your voice to try it exactly how you showed him but now every time the computer has a problem it says, "Hello, this is Tom and I am recording my voice.""

Tom, 6.17pm

"How do we take a photo of the cat?"

Marie, 6.21pm

"Can everyone on the internet see us? Tom wants to stick a piece of tape over the camera but I told him it might leave a mark."

Tom, 6.40pm

"Where do you put the batteries? I took the four screws out of the bottom panel but that wasn't it. "

Tom, 7.04pm

"Marie did something and now the pointer looks different."

Tom, 7.09pm

"It's ok now. I fixed it."

Marie, 7.16pm

"Tom changed the password to round dots."

Marie, 7.53pm

"Every time Tom clicks something in Google, do we get charged twenty-five cents?"

Marie, 8.10pm

"How do we delete the Internet? We just want the photo of the cat."

Marie, 8.35pm

"How long does it need to sleep?"

Marie, 9.20pm

"I uploaded a photo to Facebook. Have a look at it, it's hilarious. I'll wait. It's of the cat."

Marie, 9.55pm

"Tom forgot the computer was on his lap and got up to let the cat out. Now it's in Spanish."

Tennis Ball

When I was twelve, a friend of mine named Wilson invented a game called Tennis Ball.

"You know what would be an awesome game, David?"

"What?"

"Tennis, but you play it at night by dipping the tennis ball in petrol and lighting it."

"Sounds a bit dangerous."

"No, it wouldn't be. We'd wear a fireproof glove to pick the ball up with. My dad has a leather glove near our fireplace that you can pick up burning logs with."

"Well as long as we have a fireproof glove I can't see how anything could go wrong. We should call the game Fireball Tennis."

"No, we're not calling it that. I invented the game so I get to name it."

"Fine. What are we are going to call it then?"

"Something like... Fire Tennis."

"That's just my name without the ball bit."

"No it isn't, okay, what's something like a fireball but isn't the word fireball... like... a ball of fire."

"Comets are balls of fire. We could call it Comet Ball."

"I was just about to come up with that and now we can't use it. Besides, it's still tennis, we have to have the word tennis in the name... like instead of Comet Ball, it could be... Tennis Ball."

"Tennis Ball?"

"Yes, because it needs to say tennis and we play it with a ball."

"It doesn't say anything about the ball being on fire."

"It doesn't need to, we know the ball is on fire. It's my game and we're calling it Tennis Ball."

Despite the fireproof gloves, Tennis Ball was actually pretty dangerous. We may have soaked the ball for too long but I'm not sure that made a difference. Wilson slept over and we snuck out my window that night with two tennis rackets, a tennis ball, and an ice-cream container of petrol we'd drained from a leaf-blower. There were tennis courts at the end of our street; my father had been a member there for several years until he ran off with the lady that did the club fees. Lighting the tennis ball went off without a hitch and Wilson ran with it to the other side of the court to serve. Forgoing the bounce, he threw the ball high and slammed it with his tennis racket.

I definitely had the best view from my side of the court. The fireball was probably twenty feet in diameter; splashes of fire made the net. Wilson started blistering on the walk home so when we got back, he laid on the grass and I turned the sprinkler on for him.

Cloud Backgrounds

From: Walter Bowers
Date: Monday 17 August 2015 9.15am
To: David Thorne
Subject: Pay

Hey,

Did you know Jodie makes more per annum than me? Do you think I should say something to Mike?

....

From: David Thorne
Date: Monday 17 August 2015 9.19am
To: Walter Bowers
Subject: Re: Pay

Without question. I'm surprised you haven't already kicked in Mike's door and demanded an explanation. Apart from Jodie having worked here longer than you of course. How do you know her income?

David

From: Walter Bowers
Date: Monday 17 August 2015 9.25am
To: David Thorne
Subject: Re: Re: Pay

I just saw who gets what on Melissa's screen when she was getting coffee. I should be making more than Jodie the fat bitch doesn't even know how to use Photoshop. I've got a degree and she hasn't got shit. Mike's in a meeting or I would have. Should I just ask for a raise or should I say I know what Jodie gets and I should be getting at least the same as her?

....

From: David Thorne
Date: Monday 17 August 2015 9.36am
To: Walter Bowers
Subject: Re: Re: Re: Pay

Walter,

As you saw 'who gets what', you know that I also earn more than you - and a lot less than others who have been here longer.

Regardless, I think you're doing yourself a disservice by equating your worth to hers. Ignoring your inarguably superior set of skills, just having you around is worth twice Jodie's wage. However bad my day is, I can always depend on you to be having a worse one. Misery loves company and with you it's like a party. Just popping out of my office to have a quick squiz at your scowling sad head staring at the clock has gotten me through many an afternoon.

Feel free to ignore my advice but, if I were you, I'd demand a minimum of 20% over Jodie's current wage - unless of course you doubt your skills are 20% greater than hers. That way, when Mike talks you down to 10%, you still come out on top.

David

....

From: Walter Bowers
Date: Monday 17 August 2015 9.43am
To: David Thorne
Subject: Re: Re: Re: Re: Pay

I don't stare at the clock and I don't care that you make more than me, you're old. Jodie's not much older than I am. My skills are 2000% greater than hers. She doesn't know anything.

What if he says no?

From: David Thorne
Date: Monday 17 August 2015 9.52am
To: Walter Bowers
Subject: Re: Re: Re: Re: Re: Pay

Walter,

Why would Mike say no? If you provide a list of reasons - perhaps through a Power Point presentation - of why you deserve to be paid a fair amount for what you bring to the company, it would be illogical for him to anything of the sort.

I'd keep the list short, say five bullet points, to avoid repeating and diffusing your strengths. 'Misery party' is the same as 'Happiness vacuum' so don't use both. Focus on five defined strengths that you feel confident discussing further if prompted. It's pretty standard stuff.

Also, I'd strike while the iron's hot.

I know Mike has meetings all day but he breaks for lunch at twelve so that would probably be the best time to catch him. Do you think you could have a presentation ready by then?

It shouldn't take you long to set up the projector.

David

From: Walter Bowers
Date: Monday 17 August 2015 9.59am
To: David Thorne
Subject: Re: Re: Re: Re: Re: Re: Pay

Single screen or presentation?

From: David Thorne
Date: Monday 17 August 2015 10.04am
To: Walter Bowers
Subject: Re: Re: Re: Re: Re: Re: Re: Pay

A five screen presentation with animated page swipes and *boing* noises would obviously best showcase your talents but, as you only have a couple of hours, I'd suggest content and layout as priorities.

David

From: Walter Bowers
Date: Monday 17 August 2015 10.32am
To: David Thorne
Subject: Re: Re: Re: Re: Re: Re: Re: Re: Pay

Something like this?

From: David Thorne
Date: Monday 17 August 2015 10.38am
To: Walter Bowers
Subject: Re: Re: Re: Re: Re: Re: Re: Re: Re: Pay

Looks good.

I'd make the key words (paid, degree, experience, quickly,
unattended, knowledge, skills) in bold as well though.

Also, change the dots to checkboxes and add another
question mark.

David

From: Walter Bowers
Date: Monday 17 August 2015 10.57am
To: David Thorne
Subject: Re: Re: Re: Re: Re: Re: Re: Re: Re: Re: Pay

Why does **Walter** deserve to be **paid** more than Jodie???

- ☑ I have a **degree** in graphic design
- ☑ I have **experience** in Photoshop and Illustrator
- ☑ I work **quickly**
- ☑ I can work **unattended**
- ☑ I bring **knowlege** and **skills** to the company

From: David Thorne
Date: Monday 17 August 2015 11.03am
To: Walter Bowers
Subject: Re: Re: Re: Re: Re: Re: Re: Re: Re: Re: Re: Pay

Walter,

That's looking a lot better but when I said checkboxes, I had more of a chart thing in mind. A comparison between your strengths and Jodie's. The current layout allows one to question, "Yes, but which of these strengths does Jodie also have?" I'd make it a bit more obvious that she has none.

Also, as your five key points are meant to be strengths, not essays, I'd lose everything but the words in bold. The more simple you make it, the less there will be to explain.

The word 'quickly' won't work like that so change it to 'speedy' and change unattended to 'untenable' - they mean the same thing.

The word 'why' in the title is also a bit superfluous. The whole title is superfluous really.

I'd remove it and just have a large VS between your names. It will be a lot cleaner.

Also, if you wanted to push a point, you could have Jodie's name written in Comic Sans. It will add a subtle visual statement regarding her lack of typographic experience. That's up to you though.

David

....

From: Walter Bowers
Date: Monday 17 August 2015 11.08am
To: David Thorne
Subject: Re: Re: Re: Re: Re: Re: Re: Re: Re: Re: Re: Re: Pay

Checkboxes like a chart?

From: David Thorne
Date: Monday 17 August 2015 11.12am
To: Walter Bowers
Subject: Re: Re: Re: Re: Re: Re: Re: Re: Re: Re: Re: Re: Re: Pay

Yes, exactly. Unless you'd prefer a bar graph.

Also, add a cloud background.

....

From: Walter Bowers
Date: Monday 17 August 2015 11.35am
To: David Thorne
Subject: Re: Re: Re: Re: Re: Re: Re: Re: Re: Re: Re: Re: Re: Re: Pay

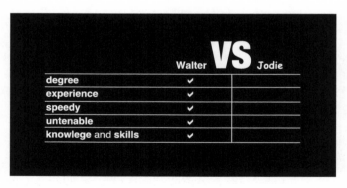

Not sure about a cloud background.

From: David Thorne
Date: Monday 17 August 2015 11.39am
To: Walter Bowers
Subject: Re: Re: Re: Re: Re: Re: Re: Re: Re: Re: Re: Re: Re: Re: Re: Pay

Walter,

Mike likes cloud backgrounds and you only get one first impression.

One issue though, 'experience' and 'knowledge & skills' are the same thing so I would change 'knowledge & skills' to 'understanding' and change 'experience' to 'wisdom'. Also, change 'degree' to 'equipped'.

Once you've made these changes, it should be good to go.

David

....

From: Walter Bowers
Date: Monday 17 August 2015 11.51am
To: David Thorne
Subject: Re: Re: Re: Re: Re: Re: Re: Re: Re: Re: Re: Re: Re: Re: Re: Re: Pay

I had to reverse the type because you couldn't see it otherwise. I haven't got time to make any more changes and I think it looks pretty good.

	Walter VS Jodie	
equipped	✓	
wisdom	✓	
speedy	✓	
untenable	✓	
understanding	✓	

I could make the lensflare a bit brighter though.

From: David Thorne
Date: Monday 17 August 2015 11.53am
To: Walter Bowers
Subject: Re: Re: Re: Re: Re: Re: Re: Re: Re: Re: Re: Re: Re: Re: Re: Re: Re: Pay

I wouldn't mess with perfection. I'd say good luck but you won't need it.

David

From: Walter Bowers
Date: Monday 17 August 2015 11.56am
To: David Thorne
Subject: Re: Re: Re: Re: Re: Re: Re: Re: Re: Re: Re: Re: Re: Re: Re: Re: Re: Re: Pay

Thanks.

....

From: Mike Campbell
Date: Monday 17 August 2015 12.37pm
To: David Thorne
Subject: Walter's timesheets

David, can I see you in my office when you have a moment?

Mike

Things

Holly pretends she doesn't have any 'things that she does'. Things that are annoying. She actually has several 'things' but I won't list them all here. Because I'm kind and respectful, not because I can't think of any. Apparently I have a lot of 'things' and a quick skim through Holly's foreword reveals highly exaggerated examples. Some people need to put down others to feel better about themselves and, as is usually the case, those blind to their own imperfections display them far more boldly than those of us who accept and work around them.

As far as 'things' go, yelling at people on the television may not seem like a big 'thing' but Holly yells at people on the television *a lot*. She once yelled at a woman on television for wearing a puffy jacket. I mentioned to Holly recently that yelling at people was one of her 'things' and she replied, "What are you talking about? I've never yelled at the television in my life."

Writing down everything Holly yelled during a week of television, I actually went through two pocket-notepads. The following are just highlights.

Jeopardy

"Oh my god, Sarah. You're on *Jeopardy* and that's the best story you could come up with? That you caught a train in Pakistan? Nobody gives a fuck."

"Shut up Alex, you condescending Canadian dick. You only know the answer because you have the answer written on a card."

"Mongolia? Oh my god, you stupid cow. Mongolia doesn't have a double T in it."

"Nice cardigan, Roger!"

"You have to phrase it as a question Vest Boy. Shaking your head doesn't change anything. Learn the rules or fuck off back to Pennsylvania."

"How did you even get on this show, Brenda? Do you have a friend that works there? Did you just sneak in?"

"Make it a true daily double, Brian!"

"Drawing a flower instead of a dot in your name doesn't make you cute, Vicky. Nothing will."

"What is Aleve!"

"Were you in a rush to get to the studio Dennis? Nobody had a brush you could borrow?"

"Don't get too cocky Sarah, you train riding fuck. It was an easy question. You're not all that."

"Please. You couldn't iron your shirt, Matt?"

Wheel of Fortune

"It's 'warming' the oven you dumb fuck. Not 'burning'. Why would you burn an oven?"

"Just solve the puzzle, Jenny. It's for a trip. What are you doing? Don't spin again... See, that's what happens you crazy eyed homeless woman. Now the fat fuck on the end gets to go to Mexico."

"A walk in the dark, Paula? Really? That's a phrase in your house is it? Someone asks you if something is difficult and you tell them 'No, it's a walk in the dark'? Why don't you go for a walk in the dark. And get murdered."

"Yes, that's right Stephanie, give yourself a little clap you flabby fish-faced prostitute."

The Great Race

"Oh my god Susan, just paint the wooden giraffe already."

Commercials

"Okay Bob. Enough. Nobody wants your ugly sofa set for $799 even if it does come with a free ottoman. It looks like you stole it off the front porch of a crack house."

"Shut up you little whore, you don't need that many snacks for the girl scout meeting."

"Nobody cares about trivago.com, just give it up. It's a stupid name and you look like a child molester. Especially when you do that wink and point thing... that's the one."

"Eight dollars? I've seen them for six at Target you thieving pirate king."

Flea Market Flip

"Gorgeous is hardly the word I'd use to describe a piece of chipboard glued to a stack of wheel rims, Lara. I wouldn't put that in a house full of squatters."

"Yes, you're very creative Jamie. You should take this up full-time. There's probably a huge market for lamps made out of traffic cones."

"Don't do it, moron. You're going to have serious buyer's remorse when you stop the car on the way home and leave it on the side of the road."

The Walking Dead

"Get a haircut, Carl. Or put the hat back on. Where is that hat? Have you lost it?"

"Quick Darryl. Grab a stick!"

The Meadows

"The name is a bit deceptive, Holly. The word meadow implies some kind of field vegetated by grass and other non-woody plants, not trucks, Confederate flags and child molestation."

"There's a field over there."

"That's an airport."

"It's still a field."

"Technically, yes. Not somewhere you'd take the family for a picnic though. I'm going home."

"I promised Ina we'd go to her barbecue, so we're going."

"It's a trailer park. I'm going to be stabbed and you're going to be chained in a shipping container."

"It doesn't look that bad. Look, that trailer has Christmas decorations. With a giant inflatable snowman."

"It's June."

"We're going."

"If you make me, I'm going to sit in the car with the doors locked. I need more emotional preparation for a situation like this. And a different outfit. I'm wearing a t-shirt that says I heart squirrels. I need some kind of thin western shirt with the sleeves cut off. The kind with studs for buttons. And a Pontiac Trans-Am with a gold eagle on the hood."

"You don't like the t-shirt I got you?"

"Yes, I like the t-shirt. Not a big fan of Gildan though."

Unfortunately, Ina saw us and ran out barefooted in bike shorts and a bikini top to guide us to their trailer. I'm not sure where she found a pair of bike shorts that size but whoever sells them has a social responsibility to stop.

We parked next to red Chevy Silverado pickup truck that was lifted so high, the door handles were head height. It had a sticker on the back window that said 'Not My President!' above Obama's face with a red target over it, and a bigger sticker that said Chevrolet. So that people driving behind can tell it's a Chevrolet without having to get too close I suppose.

"What kind of pickup truck is that in front of us?"
"I'm not sure, I'll speed up and check..."
"Just be careful, the roads are icy."
"Oh, wait, it's a Chevrolet. I don't need to drive dangerously because he's got a big sticker on the back window that says Chevrolet. We should get one of those stickers for our Saturn. One that says Saturn obviously, not Chevrolet."
"Yes, we should. You can't put a price on safety."

There were four other guests at the barbecue, not including Ina's boyfriend Luke and their eight children.
One of the guests, a 400-pound man in his fifties named TNT, had one tooth, no shirt, and two crossed sticks of dynamite tattooed on his chest. I asked him what he did and he replied, "Eat pussy."

Two of the guests were Ina's parents. Her father looked like a stick insect wearing a Santa beard and her mother looked like a pudding wearing a wig. They were both deaf so I guess they met at some kind of deaf camp or something. I've got nothing against deaf people but the 'nuhugghnnn' noise gets a bit annoying and there's no point trying to teach me how to say banana with eighty sequential hand movements that look like you're conjuring a water demon because I'm not going to remember it. Just carry a pad and pencil around and either write the word banana or draw one. Also, the jazz fingers instead of clapping thing. Not a huge fan.

I worked with a deaf guy named Neil for a couple of years. He looked like a human/axolotl hybrid and had red hair so there wasn't a lot going for him. We worked in different departments - he was an account rep at Amcor while I worked in the art department - but we often had to drive to attend client meetings together. The trips were excruciating because he drove a manual hatchback and, even at highway speeds, never went above second gear. The engine screamed and the RPM gauge redlined while he sat there oblivious. Sometimes I'd try to alert him to the fact but he'd just smile and nod and say, "Nuhugghnnn." We were late for a meeting one afternoon and, after gunning his vehicle harder than usual, the engine blew up. Cylinders actually punched through the hood and flames came out the air-conditioning vents. Also, if you can't hear people knocking on your office door, perhaps lock it if you're planning on having a lunch wank.

Ina's parents lived in the trailer next door, which was probably quite handy for babysitting and Grits Sunday. Her father invited me over to look at his collection of brown slacks and showed me some kind of special video camera setup on his television for deaf people. I had to sit in a chair and wave at a deaf person in Alaska.

The fourth guest, a blonde woman wearing a hoodie with *Team Jesus* written across it, told me I talked funny and when I explained I was from Australia, she asked if I'd driven to the United States.

"No, there's actually a fair bit of water between the two countries so you'd need some kind of amphibious vehicle with a decent sized fuel tank to make it by driving."
"What?"
"You'd need an amphibious vehicle."
"What's amphibious mean?"
"Like a frog."
"TNT, this guy says he came to America on a frog."
"No I didn't."
"Have you ever seen a kangaroo?"
"Yes. Thousands."
"Can you ride them?"
"No."
"Have you ever seen an emu?"
"Yes. But it's pronounced 'eem-you' not 'ee-moo'."
"Can you ride eemooyoos?"

"What's your fascination with riding wildlife?"

"I don't have a fascination. Have you ever seen a crocodile?"

"Yes, Queensland beaches are crawling with them. And before you ask, no you can't ride them."

"Why would anyone want to ride a crocodile? Have you ever seen a dingo?"

"Holly, how long are we staying?"

"A few hours."

"Right. Don't forget we've got that thing later. That thing that we have to go to."

"There's no thing."

There were no seats outside so we all sat inside the trailer on a damp brown velour lounge suite, staring at each other and listening to a Kid Rock CD. Ina had hand painted the phrase *Live, Laugh, Love* in large script above a pot belly stove and we all agreed that it added value to the trailer and that she was like some kind of reincarnation of Gandhi.

There was also no actual barbecue but Luke had slow-cooked a large pot of bear meat stew for two days. We each had to put in five-dollars for it but, because Holly and I are vegetarian and didn't eat, we received a two-dollar discount.

When a bottle of Jim Beam was passed around to swig from - after everyone had finished the beer that Holly and I had bought - we said we were going to get more beer and drove home instead.

Later we learnt that Luke had driven to buy more alcohol, with four children in the back, and rolled his Chevrolet. He was charged with child endangerment, driving under the influence, driving with a suspended license, and driving an unregistered vehicle. He did ninety days in jail and while he was locked up, Ina slept with his brother and gave TNT a blowjob for twenty-dollars.

Clowns

Holly looked over my shoulder. "What are you writing? Is it another email correspondence?"

"No," I responded, "I'm writing an article."

"You should post another email correspondence," Holly advised, "People like the emails."

"Yes, I realise that, the problem is that when I post an email exchange, everyone says, 'oh, another email exchange' and when I post a non-email article, they say 'I like the email correspondences better. I'm like one of those clowns that twists balloons into animal shapes at children's parties."

"Is the article about clowns?" asked Holly.

"What? No. Nobody wants to read about clowns."

"They might if it was an email exchange."

"When have I ever emailed a clown?"

"How would I know? I have no idea what you get up to all day on the Internet."

"It certainly isn't corresponding with clowns."

"I can only take your word for that. What's the article about then?"

"The time I went to deer camp with JM."

"That sounds boring," Holly replied, "you should email a clown and see what he says."

Deer Camp

I met my good friend JM at a work function Holly dragged me to. It was one of those networking things that I usually manage to get out of by pretending I've hurt my back or have a toothache, but that takes some prior planning and she'd only informed me about it at the last minute.

"It's for the building association. You'll have fun, it's at a kitchen renovation company this time."

"Why would that make it any more fun, Holly?"

"There will be taps and sinks to look at. We need new fittings for Seb's bathroom."

"Seb doesn't care about bathroom fittings. All he wants in his bathroom is decent wi-fi and a lock on the door."

"We're going. You'll meet new people and you can wear that new shirt my parents bought you for your birthday."

"It gets worse every time you say something."

"Just get ready. We're leaving in ten minutes."

"What? That doesn't give me time. I need to shave and shower. I took the rubbish out today and got a bit sweaty and my hair still has a massive cocky from bed last night. You'll have to go without me."

"We're leaving in ten minutes. Just don't stand too close to anybody or turn your head to the right."

For the first hour or so, I feigned interest in sinks close to the makeshift bar. I flicked a few taps on and off and nodded as if to say, 'good tap that one, definitely a tap I'd consider buying'. There were almost fifty people standing around in small groups chatting about whatever people at building association networking events chat about - probably doors and vinyl siding - so it was fairly easy to avoid Holly who would make me meet people.

Apart from an occasional nod and smile, I'd managed to avoid most interaction when I felt a firm hand on my shoulder. "Allow me," said a man with a large, friendly smile. He reached up to the back of my shirt collar and yanked off the $12.99 price tag, handing it to me with a chuckle.

"Thanks. I've been walking around for an hour with that on. People have been looking at me strangely but I thought it was because of my hair."

"No problem, do I detect an accent?"

"Australian."

"Ah, you must be Holly's husband. She's a nice girl."

"Yes, she can be. Not all the time of course, mostly just in public or when she wants something. I'm David."

"JM."

"Nice to meet you, JM. Are you a member of the building association?"

"Yes, I'm the president."

"Nice. You must be doing alright then. Can you get me a good deal on taps?"

"Maybe. What do you do, David?"

"Have you ever been to a shopping mall and seen those motorised animals that kids pay to ride around on?"

"Yes. You run one of those?"

"No, I just ride around on the animals."

"Haha. Holly already told my wife Lori that you're a writer. Do you shoot?"

Gun ownership isn't a thing in Australia. People used to be allowed to own rifles, but some moron went berserk at a popular tourist attraction in the nineties, resulting in the introduction of some of the world's most restrictive gun legislation. Even before that I wasn't exposed to guns. There was a kid on our street who owned a BB gun but I wasn't allowed to play with him because his house had a letterbox shaped and painted like a cow. According to my father, it bought property values down and displayed a lack of refinement. Words were exchanged and letters written which resulted in bright pink teats being added.

The closest I had ever come to holding a real gun was playing *Bug Hunt* with the Atari XG-1 light gun. For those not familiar with the game, you're not missing out on much. It consisted of shooting bugs made of pixels the size of paint swatches with a gun so inaccurate, shooting at the wall gave you a higher score. The game lasted about ten minutes which included eight minutes to calibrate the gun, a minute yelling "Oh my god, this is bullshit", and a minute loading *Missile Command* instead.

"Bug Hunt?" queried JM.

'Yes, I had the high score. Just in my family though, not the highest score in the world or anything."

"What are you doing Saturday morning?"

I had no idea what to expect as I drove up the winding dirt road towards The Flying Rabbit. The road was lined by wooden fences, behind which tall corn grew, and every second fencepost had a plastic American flag stapled to it.

To be honest, I had no intention of actually going when I said I would but that Saturday morning, Holly wanted me to help her go through her wardrobe and organise it into three piles; Keeping, Maybe Keeping, and Trying On Again With Different Pants in a Minute.

"When did you arrange this?" Holly asked.

"At the faucet party on Wednesday. I said I'd go and I don't want to disappoint the guys."

"What guys?"

"I don't know, guys with guns. JM invited me. I'm meant to meet him in less than an hour."

"Are there going to be girls there?"

"Yes, thousands. Apparently the National Bikini Model Clay Shooting Championships are being held there today."

"Right, well JM is nice. He's a work client so don't say anything stupid. Is that what you're wearing?"

I only have three types of outfit; suits, pyjamas, and stuff. All of them are either black or grey so I usually just mix and match for most occasions and use the 'single pile on the floor' system for ready access. The first project Holly and I undertook when we purchased our house was to knock down a wall between our bedroom and an adjoining room to turn it into a walk-in closet, but I learnt upon completion that it was only for her to use.

The dirt road led to a parking area near a small shack and I pulled into a space between identical Chevrolet Silverado pickup trucks. One had a large confederate flag sticker on the back window, which made me doubt my decision for a moment, but it also had a sticker with a snake saying, "Dont tread on me" so I figured the owner of the vehicle couldn't be all that bad if he cared about local wildlife so much.

"Is that what you're wearing?" asked JM. He was sitting with a group of four others on the front deck of the shack. I'd heard shots as I left the car and they'd watched as I ducked behind two pickups and ran with my head down like I was boarding a helicopter the rest of the way.

I was introduced to the owner - an old guy named Rick with a red setter named Rusty - and the people I'd be shooting with that day. There were five in our party: JM, me, a dentist named Doug, a marine named Murdock, and a short chubby Indian man named Amar. I left my suit jacket and scarf in the car and donned the green size 3XL shooting vest offered.

"Fits well," JM said, "Plenty of room." He pulled tabs on the sides and the bottom of the vest flared out like a dress. "Do you have safety glasses?"

"No."

"Here," he said, handing me a pair of mirrored Aviators.

I caught a glimpse of my reflection in the window of the shack as we headed out to the course trail. I'd hoped to get photos of the day to post on Facebook which wasn't going to happen now. I'd also hoped that there would be some form of safety lesson and instructions.

"You're up at the stand," said JM, "We will give you a few practice shots before we start properly." He handed me a shotgun and a box of shells.

"So there's no safety lesson or instructions?"

"Don't shoot anybody."

"Right. And how do I put the bullets in the gun?"

"They're shells. It's an 'over under' so you push the lever to the right to open it... that's right... put two shells in, and snap it closed. Keep your finger off the trigger because it's now loaded. When you're ready, yell "Pull" and I'll press this button that sends a target flying into the air. Try to hit it. After I hear your first shot, I'll send off the second target. That's called report pairs. A true pair is when I send both targets at the same time. If you hit a target, you get an X on the scoresheet, miss and you get an O. There's 16 stations, six shots per station. Person at the end with the most X's wins. You're up."

"Do I have to remember all that?"

"No, just the part about not shooting anybody."

I was in the woods, with a group of strangers, holding a loaded weapon. I've heard that some people feel a sense of power when they hold a gun, of being in control. I felt the exact opposite. This is how accidents happen I thought, you give loaded weapons to people who have no idea what they are doing, people who have no training, people who are extremely conscious of how much their vest flares out and wished they'd helped organise a closet instead.

"Pull," I yelled.

A machine to my left made a thudthuda noise and an orange disk sailed into the air. I pulled the trigger. There was a muffled 'doof' and recoil punched me in the shoulder. I missed. Almost immediately a second disk flew up, I fired and missed again.

"Perhaps if I watch someone else do it," I suggested.

"No, you're doing fine," replied JM, "just lean into the shot, follow the clay, and relax. The trick is not to overthink it."

I reloaded, mounted the gun to my shoulder, and closed my eyes.

A few years back, the agency I worked for was commissioned to design a brochure titled *Living with Anxiety* which included a list of relaxation methods. Along with the usual breathing and physical exercise suggestions, it described a Japanese technique called *Iwa-Baransu* which requires you to close your eyes and visualise balancing a round stone on top of slightly larger round stone to form a stack against a wind. The wind's strength is determined by the issue at hand. Apparently it was a technique practiced by Samurai before battle and now more commonly before business meetings. I tried it prior to a meeting to discuss responsibility for twenty-thousand copies of the brochure being printed and sent out with 'We'll bring highkicks' listed under services offered instead of 'Well-being checkups' and have used the technique daily since.

"Are you falling asleep?"

"No Holly, tell me more about your day."

"Well, I returned her call and left a second message and she called me back an hour later while I was at lunch and left a message to call her but when I did, it went straight to messages again. As far as I'm concerned, the bitch can order her own promotional travel-mugs."

It doesn't work every time of course. Our department recently had to take part in Excel training for no apparent reason and ten minutes into the lesson, despite my stone stack reaching shoulder height, I wanted to stab everyone in the room. At one point, Joylene (a large woman from HR with four framed photos of her cats and one of her deceased father holding a trout on her desk) actually stated, "Ooo, I love Excel."

Who says, "Ooo, I love Excel."? How is it even a sentence? Each time Joylene had a question, she waved her pen, with a huge rainbow coloured feather taped to the end, above her head while making excited "uh, uh, um, uh" noises.

"Yes, Joylene?"
"If I want my columns colour coded, am I able to mix my own preferred range of blues from a palette or do I have to select from the four-thousand shades of blue it already has?"
"And that, your Honor, is when the defendant leapt across the desk. I enter into evidence the rainbow feather pen."

If there ever comes a time where I'm typing numbers into boxes and decide I'd really like those boxes with numbers to be a specific shade of blue, it will be time to turn off the computer, pack my things, and start a fire. Along with photos of cats and dead fishermen on her desk, Joylene has a vast collection of scented candles with names like Highland Bog and Tuscan Spitpig so it would be easy to make it look like it was her fault.

I opened my eyes. "Pull."

I squeezed the trigger. The disk exploded in a puff of orange dust and the group behind me exploded in cheers. In that brief moment, I understood how Olympians feel standing on a podium, how mountaineers feel looking down from a summit, how Joylene felt when told she had a good grasp of Excel basics.

I was instantly addicted. Though I completed the course with a pitiful score of seventeen percent, every hit had been front-page newsworthy and every miss evaluated for next time. Afterwards, we drank beer from the back of a Chevrolet Silverado. It was, as far as I was concerned, the greatest sport ever invented.

I bought my first gun the next day. A Browning Citori from the top rack at Dick's Sporting Goods. I also bought a cleaning kit. And a shooting vest. Then glasses and earplugs, field-carry bag, fibre-optic sight, a better shooting vest... Hours were spent on YouTube watching instructional videos. I learnt about stance, following the shot, placement, choke types and what the numbers meant on boxes of shells. The following week my score was around thirty percent, then fifty. I became good friends with JM and the others and looked forward with fervour to each game. Then it snowed and the Flying Rabbit closed for winter.

From: JM
Date: Thursday 20 Nov 2014 11.06am
To: David Thorne
Subject: Shooting

David,

What are you doing this weekend? Do you want to come shooting?

JM

From: David Thorne
Date: Thursday 20 Nov 2014 11.19am
To: JM
Subject: Re: Shooting

Hey JM,

The Flying Rabbit is closed. :(

From: JM
Date: Thursday 20 Nov 2014 12.46pm
To: David Thorne
Subject: Re: Re: Shooting

I know. We're headed up to Deer Camp tomorrow afternoon for two nights and you're more than welcome to join us. I can pick you up at 3 if you want to come, it's a three hour drive from your place.

JM

From: David Thorne
Date: Thursday 20 Nov 2014 1.08pm
To: JM
Subject: Re: Re: Re: Shooting

What's at Deer Camp?

From: JM
Date: Thursday 20 Nov 2014 1.23pm
To: David Thorne
Subject: Re: Re: Re: Re: Shooting

No phone reception and no women.

It's a large wooded property in West Virginia with trails and stands. Tent and bunks are set up, you'd just need to pack your license, warm gear and a rifle with a decent scope.

You coming?

JM

....

I bought my second gun that afternoon. A Browning Medallion 308 with Redline scope, as it matched my other gun. I should have also bought the pair of battery heated socks I saw at Dick's for $49.99.

It was cold at Deer Camp. A lot colder than I thought it would be. A deep, biting cold that was barely kept at bay by the roaring camp fire waiting for us. Murdock and Doug had arrived a few hours before us, Amar cancelled due to an issue having his hormone replacement prescription filled. I'd known him for almost three months and hadn't realised he was born a woman.

"Are you sure about that, JM?"

"Of course I'm sure, I've known him for five years and he's only been a man for two. His name used to be Aisha."

"But he always has, you know, that big bulge in the front of his trousers. It's not just the pleats. It's pretty out there."

"Overcompensation. Same thing with the way he walks. It's actually a rubber penis. A special one that he can pump up by squeezing the balls."

"Really? I'm going to ask him if I can see it."

"You can't do that."

"Why not? He'd probably be flattered that I took an interest. Have you ever seen it?"

"Yes. At Applebee's. He was using the restroom stall while I was using the urinal and I saw it drop on the floor and roll under the door."

"What did you do?"

"I kicked it back under for him."

"Are you making this up?"

"I swear to god."

"I've never been to Applebee's. Is the food any good?"

"Not bad. The quesadillas are fairly decent."

I thought I knew a transgender woman named Brooke once. Turned out she wasn't and had no idea what I was talking about when I casually bought up gender reassignment surgery one day. I'd been open-minded and accepting for three years so I was a bit pissed off that it was a complete waste of effort.

I finished my quesadilla and threw the foam container into the fire. We'd decided to stop at Applebee's on the way and pick up dinner for everyone. It wasn't as good as JM had made it out to be. I held my hands over the container as it flared up, thankful for even a small amount of additional heat.

"Do you want to borrow a beanie?" Murdock asked between mouthfuls.

"No, I look like a fisherman when I wear one. I own a wide brimmed Fedora but I didn't bring it. It's mainly just for the beach."

"What about thermal underwear and waterproof camo gear? What's in the suitcase you brought?"

"Snacks mostly. And hair product. I also bought a Keurig machine and K-cups on the off chance there might be a generator. I almost purchased a pair of battery heated socks I saw at Dick's but I put them back when I saw the price tag. They were $49.99, which is a bit steep."

"I can loan you some gear for tomorrow," said JM, "You'll need it. It's going be a lot colder than this when we get up at 5am."

"Hahaha..."

"If we're at the top of the ridge before sunrise," he continued, "you will definitely see your first deer."

"Wait, you're serious? I'll probably just sleep in then. I've seen deer before. What time are we going shooting?"

I've only ever killed two animals in my life. The first was a kangaroo that I struck while driving Seb to school several years ago. It's a common misconception that kangaroos plague Australian city streets but they do occasionally make their way into residential areas. Their numbers are similar to that of deer in the United States but deer don't bound twenty feet into the air. I've had to brake for deer a few times but you are not given that opportunity with kangaroos, they just kind of appear from above in front of you. The car was a complete writeoff. We thought the kangaroo was fine at first, as it got up and took a few wobbly hops, but then it leant back, wiggled its arms like Neo dodging bullets in the Matrix, and keeled over. Seb poked it with a stick and took a picture on his phone for Show & Tell.

The second animal I killed was a hamster named Mr Steve. I was vacuuming under Seb's bed and heard the 'thok' as something went up but I didn't realise what it was until I reversed the hose to clear the blockage. There was another 'thok' followed by a 'thud' as Mr Steve hit the wall. I was equally horrified and impressed by the distance cleared. I put him back in his cage for Seb to find later and suggested dysentery, due to the state off Seb's bedroom, as the most likely cause of death.

"I'm not shooting a deer. I thought there was going to be a course like the Flying Rabbit but more, you know, rustic. Stations made out of logs tied together or something. You said there were stands."

"Tree stands," JM replied, "it's deer camp. What did you think you'd need a rifle with a scope for?"

"I don't know, targets a long way off or something. Another game. I thought Deer Camp was just the name, like Bear Lodge or the Canary Islands. Is it lowercase or capitalized? I'm fairly sure it was capitalized in your email."

"Do you even have a license?" asked Doug.

"Yes."

"A hunting license?"

"What?"

JM sighed. "Right, we will set you up as a diversion tomorrow. I'll put you to the left of the ridge and if you see deer, shoot into the air to send them running in our direction."

"And then you'll shoot them?"

"No, we'll jump on their backs and ride them back to camp."

"Do you eat them?"

"Of course we fucking eat them."

"Fine. Straight up or on a little bit of an angle?"

"What?"

"When I fire into the air. If I shoot straight up, should I quickly run under a tree or something?"

"If you like."

If I thought it was cold that evening, 5am the next morning taught me that I had no understanding of the concept. I pulled a borrowed glove off my hand to light a cigarette and the cold bit into my fingers instantly. A wind through the valley took snow from branches, making soggy thud noises as clumps fell beyond the light of the campsite's single lantern.

Doug heated water for coffee on coals still red from the night before, JM helped Murdock unload two ATVs from a trailer attached to his Chevrolet Silverado. I was wearing a pair of JM's thermal underwear under my jeans but JM is shorter and wider than I am so it bunched at the crotch and only came to my knees. He'd also given me a camo jacket to wear over my hoodie so I looked the part from the waist up. It was far too wide and the arms only came to just past my elbows but it was warm. It had large pockets so I packed a Fruit Rollup and a packet of Cheetos along with my cigarettes and lighter. I found an unopened Hothands hand warmer and two ticket stubs from a Lynyrd Skynyrd concert in one of the pockets. I have no idea who Lynyrd Skynyrd is but if it's the type of concert you wear a camo jacket to, I doubt I'm missing out on much. It's probably the type of stuff they play at NRA membership drives and Autumn Beer & Ballad festivals. Stuff about eagles.

I'd discovered, from a 2am excursion to the outhouse through foot-deep snow, that my boots weren't waterproof. Murdock constructed a tripod out of sticks and duct tape for me to hang them from over the firepit.

I've never knowingly met a marine before meeting Murdock but if I'd known how handy marines are to have around, I might have started hanging around jetties years ago in the hope of doing so. I assume marines have something to with boats, I've seen photos of Murdock wearing the same outfit as Captain Stubing does on his. I've also seen photos of Murdock in a helicopter wearing camo, entering murky water in diving gear and deep-sea fishing in shorts. From his photos, his cool name, and his job of course, one might assume him to be a bit of a dick, but this is not the case. He's pretty macho but it's a quiet macho, if you didn't know what he did for a living, you might assume him to be a maths teacher or piano tuner. Unless, for whatever reason, you suddenly decided to attack him. I've not yet suddenly decided to attack Murdock but I've thought about it. My guess is that I would live but it would be a long recovery. I'd probably have to use those parallel bars you see people who survived bear attacks or texted while driving using to learn to walk again on television. In one report I saw, the parallel bars had been set up in a swimming pool. I'd definitely pick that if given the option.

I tied plastic shopping bags around my feet while I waited for my boots to dry. If a travelling sock salesman had wandered through the camp selling battery heated socks for $500 a pair at that moment, he'd have made a sale.

"And will you be needing batteries with those, sir?"
"They don't come with them?"
"No, sir. Special on batteries this week though. Ten percent off if you sign up for our rewards card."

I hadn't had much sleep. Before climbing into the bunk above JM's, I'd been warned about his snoring but dismissed it as wild exaggeration. Holly snores and it's never really bothered me much, I find it kind of cute. There was nothing cute about JM's snoring. It sounded like wild boars eating a dead body. Worse than the snorty gobbling noises were the gasps and sudden silences as if he'd stopped breathing.

Around 1am, I remembered I had hearing protection in my rifle case but it was far too cold to get out of my sleeping bag.

Around 2am, I discovered the quesadilla hadn't agreed with me and I had to dress and make my way out to the outhouse. Using the word 'house' in a name gives the impression of walls so really it was just an out. The out consisted of old kitchen chair, with a circle cut in the seat, placed over a hole behind a tree. As I sat in the dark with my pants around my ankles, the wind howling across my cheeks and genitals hanging through the hole, I thought about Holly at home in our warm bed. Probably with the electric blanket on six. She'd leave it on all night and forget to turn it off in the morning which is a huge waste of electricity and quite dangerous. I read somewhere that electric blankets account for 4% of all household fires.

If there *was* a fire, I'd probably get back to find she'd saved the dogs instead of anything valuable. It's the kind of thing she'd do. I'd say the things you are meant to say like, "I'm just glad everyone got out okay" and "things can be replaced" but really, the dogs have legs and if you are running out of a burning house, there's no reason not to be carrying a flatscreen television.

I forgot to grab my hearing protection before undressing and climbing back into my sleeping bag. Around 3am, I reached down and slapped JM's bald head. He opened his eyes and said, "The fuck you didn't" so I had to pretend there was a bug on him.

We headed out after breakfast. It was still dark but the ATVs had lights. Murdock and Doug shared an ATV, I sat behind JM on the other like his bitch. The trail passed a frozen lake and wound over several hills. I spent most of the journey with my face pressed against JM's back to prevent the wind freezing my eyeballs. We came to a rickety bridge spanning a small creek and parked the vehicles nearby.

"Right," said JM, breaking a small branch from a tree and drawing a map in the snow, "We walk from here. Doug and I will head up towards the top of the hill, Murdock will be on the other side, you follow this creek until it branches."
"Okay. And then what?"
"You sit still and wait."
"For how long?"
"Until noon. We'll meet back here then and head into camp for lunch. Then we'll do it again."

I'm not a huge fan of sitting. Especially sitting still. I'm not a huge fan of running about and exercising either but somewhere in the middle works. Maybe a little bit less than middle. Not everything has to be Xtreme.

I accidently attended an Xtreme thing once and it was dreadful. I agreed to join a work team on a charity-run as it was held on a work day and I assumed, based on the fitness level of my coworkers, that it would be a brisk walk, interspersed with less-brisk walking, through a park or something. I realized this wasn't the case when we arrived to discover people wearing Fitbits and neon. They were talking about 'times' and doing stretching exercises behind SUVs with bike racks. A large sign over the starting point read:

ANNUAL 5K MUD, SWEAT & CHEERS RUN!

Two of our five member team went home. Joylene from Human Resources and Kevin from Accounts guilt-tripped me into staying. None of us finished. Kevin bowed out when he got a leg-cramp within the first three minutes, Joylene fell hard and lost her glasses in mud on the first obstacle, and I was disqualified for taking a cigarette break behind a log wall. I'd made it the furthest of our team though so that's not bad. Joylene didn't speak to me for a week but I dismissed her claims of being pushed as fanciful and expecting me to stop to help find her glasses as against the rules.

"Maybe it was just a muscle twinge."

"It wasn't a muscle twinge, I know what a push feels like."

"Well, there's no point speculating about these things."

"I'm not speculating. You pushed me. I made it to the rope platform before you, so you pushed me."

"Muscle twinges can feel like a push. Besides, you wouldn't have made it across anyway. Probably better to go down at the edge where it's shallow than in the middle. Being stuck in the middle would hold up everyone behind you."

"We were last. The only person behind me was you."

"Well there you go. Muscle twinge. Alluding to anything other just makes you come off as a bit of a bad sport. I didn't complete the mud run either."

"No, but you're wearing the t-shirt that says you did."

"I got further than you."

The sun had been up for nearly an hour. I trudged through knee-deep snow in areas. The wind picked up the snow and flung it in my face so I pulled the drawstring of my hoodie tight, leaving a hole just large enough to see out of with one eye if I walked with my neck turned. To keep my boots dry, I'd wrapped silver duct-tape around them from toe to mid-calf as per Murdock's suggestion. Doug commented that they looked like robot legs and I told him that I was happy about that, because I liked robots, and that his beanie made him look like a pedophile. The tape kept snow out but having the tread covered proved slippery on the creek's bordering slopes. I fell several times and slid into the creek twice.

131

The creek wasn't overly full, mostly just leafy frozen puddles, and I walked along it where possible, looking for places to climb back up. At one point, a large fallen tree blocked the way and I had to climb up and around a small cliff to continue. From my vantage point, I could see where the creek branched a few hundred feet ahead. I heard a gunshot in the distance behind me and hurried.

The creek widened and deepened at the branch, a sheet of ice separating me from the opposite bank. I tapped at the ice with a boot and it held. To distribute my weight, I got down on my hands and knees, with my rifle slung across my back, and shimmied across. The water under the ice was only a foot or so deep but, as I was on all fours when the ice gave way, it covered my calves and knees and halfway up my thighs. There was no warning crack like you hear in movies, a chance to pause and lie flat and wiggle off or something, it just gave way.

The water actually felt warm for a moment, I'm not sure how that's possible. Perhaps it was just the nerve endings in my legs confused momentarily by the affront. They sorted it out fairly quickly. I dragged myself out of the water and attempted to ascend the steep bank but my legs were shaking uncontrollably and the duct-tape that served to keep snow out now kept water in. It was like having my feet stuck in vases. I waded clumsily along the edge of the bank, to a spot where large gnarled tree roots protruded, and used them as a ladder to make my way to the top.

The trunk of the tree above the bank had burned at some point, it was broken off at about fifteen feet up and hollowed out by fire. The inside, lined with charcoal and blown in leaves, offered some protection from the wind. I rested my rifle against the trunk and crawled inside.

There have been instances throughout my life where I was *as* miserable but I can't think of many where I was more so. I've certainly never been that cold. I watched a documentary about arctic explorers once and it said there is a point during hypothermia where you feel an enveloping warmth. I wasn't anywhere near that. Perhaps I should have climbed back down the bank and rolled about in the water for a bit.

Sticking my legs out straight allowed much of the water to drain from my taped boots. Unzipping JM's huge jacket, I pulled my knees to my chest and zipped the jacket back up around them. My gloves were soaked so I pulled them off and tucked my hands into the pockets. I'd forgotten about the Hothand's hand-warmer and actually sobbed a bit with excitement as I read the instructions on the back of the label. The front showed a hand holding a hand-warmer that was lit up like a small sun. Inside was what looked like a fat teabag. As I held the fat teabag between frozen fingers, shaking vigorously to activate the chemical reaction, it slipped from my grip and flew over the bank into the creek.

At just past eight, I had almost three hours of sitting and waiting to get through before it would be time to start heading back. I considered starting back immediately but waiting for the others at the ATVs would afford less protection than my burnt out trunk. Besides, I had a job to do. I was the diversion. The importance of the role was questionable to say the least but after eating my Rollup and half a packet of Cheetos, there wasn't much else to do. I looked through the scope of my rifle for a bit, scanning the area and making *pew pew pew* noises, jumping when the scope was filled by a giant squirrel's face. It was sitting on a branch a dozen or so feet away staring at me. I threw several Cheetos to him but he didn't eat them. I had a can of cashews in my bag back at camp and I told the squirrel I'd bring them with me next time. After a while, his staring began to annoy me so I retracted the offer and threw a stick at him.

I'd been told not to have a cigarette, for deer have an excellent sense of smell, but I had one anyway. I then built a fire at the entrance to my shelter using leaves, sticks and Lynyrd Skynyrd ticket stubs. It was a small fire, decent wood being hidden beneath a sheet of snow, but enough to bring some feeling back into my hands. With a source of heat, shelter, and a fairly good view of the area, I put my chin on my knees and waited.

Waiting for something that may or may not happen is worse than waiting in an airport or doctor's reception where eventually the flight will board or the doctor will call you through to have a look at that weird lump on your left testicle. Waiting for deer is like waiting for a bus that may or may not come after you've heard reports of a possible strike. At least I assume it is, I don't catch buses. Not because I'm a snob, but because only school children and poor people who don't own cars catch buses. People who say they catch buses for environmental reasons aren't fooling anyone but themselves. My friend Geoffrey pretends he enjoys it but if that were true he wouldn't ask for a lift everywhere. I waited for deer for about ten minutes, then I just waited for three hours to pass.

I jerked awake. It felt like I had only nodded off for a few seconds but my fire was out, the ashes covered by a light dusting of snow. Large flakes fell gently outside my shelter, some making its way through the open roof of the trunk and collecting in the folds of my jacket. The wind had stopped and the forest was eerily silent apart from a crunching sound. At the base of the tree where the squirrel had been, a deer stood eating Cheetos.

This was my chance, I thought. My chance to be a real part of the hunting party, not simply a distraction. My chance to be a part of the group instead of joining the group. I'd shoot the deer and walk out of the forest with my kill across my shoulders - or maybe dragging it as it looked pretty heavy. They'd cheer and slap me on the back and then we'd head back to camp and sit around a roaring fire. I'd tell them I tracked it or something and took the shot from hundreds of yards away, maybe mid-leap. They'd probably give me a cool nickname, like Buckslayer or Deerplugger. Okay, perhaps not Deerplugger. I'd think of a better nickname on the walk back.

I reached slowly and quietly for my rifle, flicked the safety off, and raised the stock to my shoulder. The deer's rump was facing me and, at that range, its butt-hole filled the scope. Nobody would believe my story of a long-range mid-leap kill if I shot it in the arse.

"Hey deer."

The deer raised its head, scanning the area slowly. Its gaze paused directly at me, I held perfectly still. My heart was beating astonishingly fast. Loud enough, I was sure, for the deer to hear. Through the scope, I could see my shelter reflected in the deer's shiny dark brown eyes. In camo with a coating of snow, I was just part of a burnt stump silhouetted against the white landscape. It would be quick, between the eyes; the deer wouldn't even know what happened. Snowflakes were trapped in its eyelashes.

I watched someone die once. Her name was Emma and I was holding her hand when it happened. It was late at night on a dirt road in the middle of nowhere. Four of us had been drinking in a small country town pub, fifteen miles from an area called Stockport where we all worked on a large horse riding property. It was the kind of place where schools hold overnight 'Adventure Camp' excursions. I hadn't worked there long. I was in the back seat with a guy named Michael, the oldest son of the property owners. We got on well as he had a huge collection of porn. Emma was in the front passenger seat and her boyfriend Brian was driving. We'd left the pub early because Emma and Brian were fighting. He'd been told off earlier that day by our boss for helping a young girl, twelve or so, onto her horse by clasping her bottom. There was a rule against touching bottoms and that particular rule had only been added to the rules because Brian had a habit of it.

It was raining and the dirt road was slippery. Emma yelled for him to slow down. We all did. We were doing almost double the speed limit when Brian lost control. The wheels slipped a bit and I guess he overcompensated trying to correct the car's direction.

It happened quickly. We were travelling sideways when we hit the bank of a bend. If we hadn't slid, if it hadn't been muddy, I don't see how we could have taken the bend at that speed anyway. I told the jury that during Brian's manslaughter hearing. The car flipped, rolled twice. Twice and a half really. It was like watching slow-motion footage. I heard screaming and breaking glass, watched bodies thrash back and forth, arms and legs fly up and down. The sound of the roof sliding fifty feet along the road, inches beneath my head, was deafening. Interminable. Then it stopped. It was dark and silent but for the clicking and flashing of emergency lights.

I was upside down with the seatbelt cutting into my waist. Managing to undo the buckle, I dropped onto my side. Michael did the same, landing on my head and causing my only injury. There was no glass in the windows so we crawled out. Brian was half way out of his window and Michael helped him to his feet while I knelt besides Emma's window.

Emma was still upside down but had slipped through her seatbelt. Her arm was trapped under the roof, it must have flung out as the car flipped and been caught. Sliding along the road had taken most of the flesh from it and ripped the bone from her shoulder. It was only held on by a few inches of meat and stretched skin. Blood poured from what looked like a fat hollow pasta noodle. I pinched the pasta noodle closed between my thumb and index finger and pressed my palm against the exposed meat surrounding it. Emma cried out, looking up at me frightened. She tried to pry my hand away with her free one. I grabbed it and held it away.

"You're bleeding," I told her, "I'm just trying to stop it."
"Am I going to die?"
"No, don't be ridiculous. Your arm is a bit fucked up though."
"Is it in my hair?" she asked.
"The blood? Yes."
Her long blonde hair hung in a growing pool on the roof of the car. There seemed to be an awful lot of it.
"Fuck. I straightened it today."
Brian knelt down beside us. "Are you okay, Emma?" he asked. His eyes widened and he put his hand over his mouth.

Vomit sprayed out between his fingers, splashing the side of my face and neck as he stood and stepped back.

Michael took his place, staring at Emma's arm and putting his hand on my back.

"I'll go and get help," he said.

This was before mobile phones were a thing. They existed, but came with a case that you carried over your shoulder with a strap and only American businessmen on television had them.

"Okay, be quick. And take him with you." I nodded towards Brian who was twenty feet away, punching a speed limit sign. I heard Michael yell something at Brian, watched them sprint off down the road. Brian stopped and ran back. "I don't have my license," he said, "Will you tell them that you were the one driving?"

"Go and get help, Brian."

"But will you?"

"No."

He called me a cunt, then turned and chased after Michael, disappearing in the darkness.

"Are you alright?" Emma asked.

"Me? I'm fine. Just a bit of a headache. Everyone's fine but you. Didn't anyone ever tell you to keep your arms inside the vehicle at all times?"

"Is that a joke?"

"It was meant to be. Sorry."

"That's okay. Am I going to lose my arm?"

"I don't know. Maybe they can stitch it back on. Does it hurt?"

"Not really. It just feels cold. Brian will leave me if I only have one arm."

"Brian doesn't deserve you with two arms. Besides, if you do lose your arm, you can get a robot one. That would be pretty cool. I'd swap an arm for a robot one."

Blood was leaking through my fingers, running down my arm and dripping from my elbow. I was still holding her other hand.

"Emma, I'm going to let go of your hand because I need to use mine, okay?"

"No," she tightened her grip.

"Alright, I'm going to press harder then. Does that hurt?"

"No but you're runnnn nyr hoodie."

"Sorry?"

"Ruining your hoodie. M sorry. M really tired."

"It's an old hoodie and I don't think you are meant to go to sleep. They'll be back soon. It will probably take them twenty minutes to get into town and another ten for the ambulance to arrive. Talk to me until they get here. What kind of music do you like? Who's your favourite band?"

Back then, at that age, most conversations could be started by asking what kind of music the person listened to. The type of music you embraced defined aspects of who you were, how you dressed, who your friends were. It was simpler. In your forties, you can't just walk up to people at networking functions and chat about your favourite bands. You have to talk about bathroom fittings and look at photos on their phone of the firepit they just completed.

It's harder to make friends as the years pass but when you do, they're better ones. Or maybe you just get better at fucking things up less.

I meant to ask Brian at Emma's funeral who her favourite band was, as she hadn't answered, but he wasn't there. The crematorium played Lou Reed's *Perfect Day* during the eulogy but I don't know who picked it. When Emma's parents asked if she had said anything before she died, I told them she had apologised for getting blood on my hoodie. They nodded and hugged me as if this was somehow an acceptable answer. I didn't tell them that Emma urinated and defecated when she died. That she hadn't just gone to sleep, she'd convulsed. That her large brown eyes were open and I tried to close them but my fingers were covered in mud and blood and I got it all over her face. That I didn't know what to do so I just sat in the mud holding her hand, long after she loosened her grip. Facebook listed Brian under 'people you might know' a few years back, his profile photo showed him riding a jet ski.

I waved as I approached the ATVs. I was late returning and received half-hearted waves in response. Nobody cheered or slapped me on the back. Nobody called me Doedecker.

"Nothing?" JM asked.
"No, I saw a squirrel though. A fat one. It would probably have made a good stew."

141

"Well, that's hunting. Sometimes you get lucky and sometimes you don't. Maybe we'll all have better luck this afternoon."

We didn't go back out that afternoon, it started snowing heavily so JM, Doug and Murdock packed up camp while I wandered around pretending to look like I was doing something. I asked a few times if anybody needed a hand, just to appear helpful, but people kept saying yes so I stopped. I don't mind the whole 'adventure' thing of camping but I'm not that keen on packing up things. To be honest, I'd rather just leave it all there and buy new stuff next time.

I was invited out to deer camp a few times after that but I had to work or go faucet shopping. The photos Murdock posted on Facebook showed the group having fun. There was one of him doing a wheelie on an ATV and another of him chopping wood without a top on. They'd built a larger firepit, using stone from the creek, and added a cast iron pole to hang pots from. I left a comment under the photo saying it looked great and JM replied that "it might even be large enough now to keep you warm" which was nice.

Another photo showed JM standing beside the carcass of deer. It was strung from a tree by its hind legs. I zoomed in on the eyes to see if it was the one I had hand-fed Cheetos. They were cloudy and dull so I don't think it was.

The Flying Rabbit opened again last weekend. It was still cold but not bitingly so. I took gloves but didn't need them. Despite not having practiced for a few months, I shot well. Not as well as the others in our group but still my highest score yet at eighty-five percent. I received a few cheers and a slap on the back. Afterwards, we drank beer from the back of a Chevrolet Silverado and I asked Amar if I could see his rubber penis but he said no.

Marketing

I know several people in marketing. They're all dreadful. Somehow every discussion, regardless of topic, turns to results of their recent Facebook ad campaign for sandals made by the tribal women of Klokloklowok or Bedazzled iPhone covers.

A hundred years ago, they'd have been selling pencils on a street corner. After clocking off, they'd huddle in sad dirty groups to discuss the merits of using a smaller tin to make the pencils seem bigger.

One person I know in marketing, a crazed looking flabby woman in her thirties named Rian, could be the poster child for Dunning–Kruger effect -- a cognitive bias wherein unskilled individuals suffer from illusory superiority, mistakenly assessing their ability to be much higher than is accurate.

Devoid of any defining talent or clue and producing work that parents wouldn't put on a fridge, Rian is at a loss to understand why her Facebook campaigns for pipecleaner hair-ties aren't required reading in university courses, and why the tree she painted on her living room wall three years ago isn't displayed at the Museum of Modern Art.

Having confidence in one's abilities is a good thing but just because a dog wants to sit in the driver's seat, it doesn't mean it's capable of driving a eighteen-wheeler or school bus.

While I'm sure many find worth in the services marketing people provide, given a choice between benefits gained from two hour meetings about Adwords campaign statistics or a bucket of warm spit, I'd take the bucket of warm spit. A direction, decision or point being reached in a marketing meeting is a far less likely scenario than finding myself in a position where I need to demonstrate centrifugal force to a group of young children.

From: Pauline Olsen
Date: Monday 27 April 2015 10.12am
To: David Thorne
Subject: Book signing dates

Hello David,

It's been bought to my attention that a list of upcoming book signing events was recently posted on your website with B&N stores named as venues.

I was wondering if I could have the contact details of your agent or marketing person or if you could forward this email to them as a matter of urgency.

We have the ISBN in our system but no record of the listed events. I've spoken with two other stores and they have no record either.

Thank you, Pauline

....

From: David Thorne
Date: Monday 27 April 2015 11.02am
To: Pauline Olsen
Subject: Re: Book signing dates

Hello Pauline,

Thank you for your email. I'm currently without an agent or marketing person. I blame their inability to take criticism.

I was signed with LA based agency ICM Partners regarding television rights but after receiving a draft script, penned apparently by throwing a keyboard into a box full of squirrels and running the results through a quick spell-check, I stopped responding to their Skype group video chat requests. What was originally a satirical expose of the design industry somehow turned into a story about a mechanic named Greg. It's possible that I may have missed an artistic and clever point, but just as possible that somewhere Greg is wondering how they could have fucked up his eight part transmission rebuild series so badly.

Penguin represent my first book but my marketing person there is a small angry Asian woman who yells a lot so I have her number blocked. One might suggest marketing consists of more than the author tweeting links to his book every fifteen minutes but one would be wrong. And ungrateful. And should tweet more. We haven't spoken since she accused me of stealing a three-foot cardboard cut-out penguin from her office the last time I was there.

Incidentally, Penguin employs a similar system to ICM in regards to calculating royalties - except instead of a keyboard and squirrels, they throw a calculator into an empty box and jiggle it a bit. This is after thirty-six meetings regarding what kind of box to use, three-hundred emails discussing who will do the jiggling, and a six month delay due to pigeons, or hats, or static electricity.

Regards, David.

From: Pauline Olsen
Date: Monday 27 April 2015 11.28am
To: David Thorne
Subject: Re: Re: Book signing dates

Hello David,

Thank you for getting back to me so quickly.

Who arranged the book signing dates and who at B&N did they speak with?

Pauline

....

From: David Thorne
Date: Monday 27 April 2015 11.35am
To: Pauline Olsen
Subject: Re: Re: Re: Book signing dates

Hello Pauline,

There was no arrangement as such. I thought I'd just show up on the day. I have my own fold-up chair and table.

Regards, David.

From: Pauline Olsen
Date: Monday 27 April 2015 12.51pm
To: David Thorne
Subject: Re: Re: Re: Re: Book signing dates

You posted several venues and dates without anyone at B&N knowing anything about it?

You can't just show up. That's not how it works. There are procedures. You have to contact individual stores well in advance. If the store agrees to you doing a signing, copies need to be ordered, a date set, and arrangements made.

If you had a marketing person, they would have explained all this to you.

Pauline

....

From: David Thorne
Date: Monday 27 April 2015 1.19pm
To: Pauline Olsen
Subject: Re: Re: Re: Re: Re: Book signing dates

Hello Pauline,

Yes probably. They'd also explain cost per conversion statistics, demographic expansions and response rate ratios. They can't help themselves. It's like an involuntary tic or a really boring form of Tourette's.

149

I once attended a marketing meeting where people talked about Adwords campaign statistics for two hours. Which, in my opinion, is about one hour and fifty-six minutes too long to talk about anything. At around the forty minute mark, I honestly thought I was going to die.

In regards to procedures, I just figured it was better to be told off than told no. Seeking permission involves far more variables than pretending you didn't think there'd be an issue.

Besides, it's sitting on a chair. If it was possible to measure the difference between sitting on a chair and sitting on a chair by prior arrangement, nobody would. If someone did, everyone else would state, "That was a bit pointless. Don't you have anything better to do?"

I don't require books ordered as I'm not expecting a crowd. I'll have a couple with me just in case but, to be honest, I'm only popping in for a bit so I can claim my holiday flights as a business expense.

If anyone asks, I'll just say I spoke to Pauline and she said it's fine.

Regards, David.

From: Pauline Olsen
Date: Monday 27 April 2015 1.43pm
To: David Thorne
Subject: Re: Re: Re: Re: Re: Re: Book signing dates

Except I didn't say it's fine and the end result certainly won't be the same because you'll be asked to leave. I can't imagine anything more embarrassing.

Pauline

....

From: David Thorne
Date: Monday 27 April 2015 2.26pm
To: Pauline Olsen
Subject: Re: Re: Re: Re: Re: Re: Re: Book signing dates

Hello Pauline,

That's understandable, the day to day stress of chair allocation and authorisation probably leaves little time for such things.

I was once escorted off a plane shortly after boarding due to an ex-girlfriend calling the airport and stating I had four-hundred ecstasy tablets hidden in my bottom. Refusing to leave my seat without an explanation, two large men in suits carried me out horizontally. I was travelling with coworkers and the regional manager of BHP Billington.

A few feet from the exit, the men had to wait for someone to be seated. I was head height with other passengers and an elderly lady leaned forward and said, "It's going to be ok. You're going to get the help you need now. It's a good thing."

I was also asked to leave a restaurant once. Experiencing stomach problems and discovering the restroom toilet bowl bogged and overflowing with paper and faeces, I made an emergency decision to poo in the hand-towel disposal bin instead. With hindsight, I should have either used the ladies restroom or locked the door.

Also, when I was about twelve, my mother opened the bathroom door without knocking and caught me lying naked on the floor cracking an egg onto my penis. I have no idea why. I tried to flip over to hide my shame but the tiles were pretty slippery from several previously cracked eggs so I just kind of slapped and flailed for a bit. She didn't say anything, just closed the door, so I guess that story didn't really have anything to do with being asked to leave places.

Regardless, on an embarrassment scale of one to twenty (with one being a bit sunburnt and twenty owning a Nissan Cube), being told, "I'm sorry sir, B&N has a strict rule regarding people sitting in chairs, I'll have to ask you to leave," would probably only be a three. Maybe a four if there is jostling.

Regards, David.

From: Pauline Olsen
Date: Monday 27 April 2015 3.55pm
To: David Thorne
Subject: Re: Re: Re: Re: Re: Re: Re: Re: Book signing dates

People are allowed to sit in chairs but they aren't allowed to set up desks or sign books inside the store without permission.

You're going to have to cancel the dates you posted and go through the proper channels to set up new dates. Do you understand this?

Pauline

....

From: David Thorne
Date: Monday 27 April 2015 4.02pm
To: Pauline Olsen
Subject: Re: Re: Re: Re: Re: Re: Re: Re: Re: Book signing dates

Hello Pauline,

Mostly. Would sitting on a chair, no desk, asking people walking past if they'd like to come outside and buy a book from the back of my rental car be acceptable? Am I allowed to hold a sign?

Regards, David.

From: Pauline Olsen
Date: Monday 27 April 2015 4.13pm
To: David Thorne
Subject: Re: Re: Re: Re: Re: Re: Re: Re: Re: Re: Book signing dates

No it isn't acceptable. I'm not sure how to make this any clearer.

You do not have permission to promote your book in B&N stores or interact with B&N customers in any way. If you do, you'll be asked to leave. If you refuse to leave, the police will be called to escort you from the premises

Pauline

....

From: David Thorne
Date: Monday 27 April 2015 4.20pm
To: Pauline Olsen
Subject: Re: Re: Re: Re: Re: Re: Re: Re: Re: Re: Re: Book signing dates

Hello Pauline,

What if I stand quietly in an aisle, or a corner at the back of the store, looking at books on shelves and occasionally nodding to myself thoughtfully?

Regards, David.

From: Pauline Olsen
Date: Monday 27 April 2015 4.26pm
To: David Thorne
Subject: Re: Re: Re: Re: Re: Re: Re: Re: Re: Re: Re: Re: Book signing dates

That would make you a customer. As long as you aren't communicating with other customers in any way, I can't see that being a problem.

Pauline

....

From: David Thorne
Date: Monday 27 April 2015 5.17pm
To: Pauline Olsen
Subject: Re: Re: Re: Re: Re: Re: Re: Re: Re: Re: Re: Re: Book signing dates

Hello Pauline,

I'm glad a compromise could be reached. I have amended the previously posted event page to reflect the agreed changes.

I've also attached the promotional poster. I'll have some with me on the day but I thought you might want to print extra copies for the store windows or something.

Regards, David

From: Pauline Olsen
Date: Tuesday 28 April 2015 9.32am
To: David Thorne
Subject: Re: Re: Re: Re: Re: Re: Re: Re: Re: Re: Re: Re: Re: Re: Book signing dates

You do not have permission to attend B&N stores on the dates you have indicated.

Watching Netflix
with Holly

"Why do you always get to select the movie we watch, David?"

"Because I prefer being entertained for two hours over being drawn into a pit of despair."

"What's that supposed to mean? I pick good movies."

"You pick dramas about women struggling to overcome things nobody cares about."

"Wow. That's a fairly misogynistic comment."

"No it isn't, I don't want to watch movies about men talking about their feelings either."

"I'm picking the movie. We're watching *Precious*."

"Fine. What's it about?"

"A sixteen-year-old, overweight, sexually abused black girl who lives in Harlem during the 80s. She's on welfare and has a child with Down syndrome."

"Right."

"And she catches aids."

Watching Anything with Seb

"There's no way that pickup truck would be able to outrun a pyroclastic cloud."

"Oh my god, Seb, I don't talk all the way through movies that you want to watch."

"Yes you do, you complain non-stop. I'm going to look up how fast a pyroclastic cloud travels..."

"Just let me watch the fucking movie."

"... A pyroclastic cloud travels 450 miles per hour."

"I don't care, stop saying pyroclastic cloud. Besides, it may leave the volcano at 450 miles per hour but it would slow down as it gets further away."

"They're right next to the volcano."

"No they're not, Seb. They've been driving for ages. They just passed through a town."

"Yes, at 450 miles per hour apparently. It's probably some kind of land speed record. I'm looking it up..."

"They're not going 450 miles per hour. Look the pyroclastic cloud is catching up to them."

"763 miles per hour is the land speed record. At Black Rock Desert in a car with two Rolls Royce jet engines. Is that Sarah Conner?"

"What? Yes, but you're making me miss bits. I have no idea how they ended up in the mineshaft now. I'll have to rewind it..."

"They drove in and crashed to escape the pyroclastic cloud. And they'd be dead if they crashed going 450 miles per hour. You know what we should do?"

"Shut the fuck up and watch the movie?"

"No, stick *three* Rolls Royce jet engines on a car and break the land speed record. We could stick them on that pickup truck as it's already pretty zippy."

Watching Jeopardy With People Who Are Going Deaf

Alex Trebek: "Botanically, a peanut isn't a nut but one of these, like a soybean."

Me: "Legume."

Holly's father: "Legume."

Me: Throws hands up as if to say, "What the fuck?"

Contestant: "What is a legume."

Alex Trebek: "Correct."

Holly's father: Nods head wisely.

Repeat.

44-Gallon Drum

My offspring Seb and I purchased a 44-gallon drum from a guy on Craigslist last autumn. We drilled a dozen or so holes in the side, packed it with dead leaves, and, after instructing Seb to add a splash of fuel from a jerry can, I went inside to get a lighter.

"How much fuel did you put in?"
"A splash."
"The jerry-can is empty."
"A decent splash."

I expected a 'whoompf' but I didn't expect the volume, or for the drum to act like a cannon. Burning leaves shot high into the air and rained down over a four hundred foot radius. There was a fair amount of screaming and running. Seb lost a new t-shirt to a burn hole, which he was rather upset about, but I refused to drive him to the mall to replace it.

"We have to go, Pacsun will sell out of these shirts and I'll never find another one with pineapples on the pocket."
"You should have thought about that before dumping several gallons of fuel into the 44-gallon drum. I'm not leaving the house for four or five weeks."
"Oh my god, Dad, it's not even that noticeable. Just draw on

eyebrows with a marker and wear a hat."

"Yes, that's an excellent suggestion, Seb. Perhaps a snappy vest and a cane to complete the ensemble."

"Your hair's not even that bad. Just short at the front."

"I have *no* hair at the front. It's just little frizzle-balls. I look like an old Chinese man that works on a wharf. All I need is a couple of big sacks on my back."

"Shave it all off then. You'll look like Jason Statham."

"You really think so?"

"...Sure."

The problem is that some people's heads are Jason Statham shaped and others are concentration camp prisoner shaped. You never really know what shape your head is, or how white, until you go #0 with a set of Wahl dog grooming clippers. I'd watched a movie a few nights before, called *The Descent*, about a group of women who go spelunking without spare flashlight batteries and get chased by pale, bald humanoid creatures that live in the dark. I watched it by myself and there were a lot of jump scares, which explains why, for two or three days after shaving my head, I'd yell and go all wobbly whenever I passed a mirror.

"I don't look anything like Jason Statham."

"Yes, you do. If he had no muscles and was maybe sick or something."

"If he was sick?"

"Cancer or something. Can we go to Pacsun now?"

Later, we learned our neighbor Carl had recorded the entire 'rain of fire' incident on his phone and presented the video during that week's sub-division HOA meeting. Apparently it's against the rules to burn rubbish in your backyard because a horse burnt to death in 1876. The fine is a shiny shilling or forfeiture of your least-unattractive daughter to the town's elders. There are also ordinances covering pitching your neighbor's well, rolling your sleeves above the elbow while churning butter, and, for the record, mowing your lawn after 7pm and before 9am. Also, nobody's allowed to own chickens.

Conveniently, Carl is the president of our sub-division HOA and there are only two other members: Carl's short, round, curly-haired wife Toni, who seconds every motion, and Janice Roberts, a 93 year-old semi-mobile corpse from across the street who owns chickens and has a large sign in her front yard that states, *Though I may stumble, I will not fall, for the Lord upholds me with his hand. Psalms 37:23.* Which is false, as I've seen Janice fall at least three times. Despite a decade or two of using a walker, it's as though each outing is the first time she's ever seen one; there's no 'lift, place, step, repeat' rhythm, its just random flailing and clanking. I saw her using it upside down once, she was holding onto the tennis balls. On one occasion, she somehow managed to throw the walker twenty feet ahead, fell, and couldn't get up for several minutes. I would have eventually helped but a UPS driver stopped and lifted her off the road before I finished my coffee.

According to the written warning I received - signed, countersigned and witnessed by Carl, Toni and Janice - it was the sixth recorded instance of Seb and I breaking HOA ordinances. Some of Carl's earlier work included, *Thorne's riding ATVs on the road*, *Thorne's feeding raccoons*, and, my personal favourite, *Thorne's rolling a log down a hill into a creek*.

I emailed the HOA my own video footage (an animated gif titled *Carl_sucking_horse_cock*) but they didn't respond.

Machete Reef

Machete Island

Papua New Guinea

Machetetown

Port Machete

Macheteborough

Machete River

Machete Bay

Machete City

Macheteopolis

Macheteville

Macheteburg

Machetes and Mats

Papua New Guinea is a sparsely populated tropical country, about the same size as Turkmenistan, a hundred or so miles from Australia's northernmost tip of Queensland. It's been said that during low tide you could wade from Australia to Papua New Guinea but you'd have to be a pretty quick wader to make it there before the tide came back in so it's a stupid thing to say. I could probably wade two hundred feet before my legs got tired and I never go deeper than my knees. I've heard that sharks can still attack you in water that shallow but I'd rather be bitten on a knee than the stomach or groin. A few years back, a guy I knew in Adelaide waded out waist deep to retrieve a poorly thrown Frisbee and a shark tore off his left buttock. He survived but he has to use a little half-seat cushion to sit without leaning.

I wouldn't even go knee deep in Queensland, the water there is approximately 20% crocodile. They're salt-water crocodiles so essentially sharks with legs. I read about a woman whose poodle was taken by a salt-water crocodile while she was walking it along the beach. They were several feet from the shoreline but the crocodile exploded out of the water and closed the distance in a fraction of a second. It was a relatively small crocodile, only seven or eight feet, but even the babies can do some damage. To her credit, the woman refused to let go of the leash even after the poodle was ripped in half. She ended up with the head and front half so technically she won the tug'o'war but it wasn't much of a prize. I probably would have let the crocodile have it at that stage. Less to clean up.

If you *were* inclined to wade to Papua New Guinea, you'd need to be a sprint-wader *and* adept at fighting off salt-water crocodiles. You'd also need enough energy left over once you got there to outrun the tribes-people with machetes. Machete is the official language of Papua New Guinea. Screaming as you're hacked to death with a machete is the official second language.

As far as vacation activities go, being hacked to death with a machete isn't most people's first choice and, as such, Papua New Guinea's tourism industry is pretty much nonexistent. I'd rather visit Yemen or West Virginia than Papua New Guinea and I have no desire to hang around with angry bearded men wearing suit jackets in rubble *or* be Billy-Ray's shipping container sex slave.

My friend JM is from West Virginia and while he's generally quite personable, you do occasionally see a hint of the shipping container thing peeking through the thin veneer. Once, while we were camping, he told me that he had a pig when he was young and when I asked if it was his girlfriend, he replied, "You do realize nobody knows you're out here with me, don't you?"

I laughed but JM didn't even smile. He just spat out his tobacco and went to bed so I must have touched a raw nerve. Love is love though; I'm not one to judge. When I was eight, I had a relationship with one of my sister's dolls. It was a four-foot tall Snow White doll that looked a lot like a girl at my school named Emma Jenkins. I never had sex with the doll but I kissed it a lot and told it that I loved it. I did almost consummate the relationship one afternoon, when my parents took my sister to a soccer match, but the other team forfeited and my parents returned early to discover Snow WHite and I naked in bed. I never saw Snow White again and I had to have 'the talk' that evening. My mother also borrowed a book from the library titled *What's Happening to Me? An Illustrated Guide to Puberty* and left it in my room with a sticky-note that said, "You're normal."

I've only ever met one person from Yemen, he owned a local falafel shop until he was arrested for riding a scooter drunk and deported for being in the country illegally. He's probably standing in rubble wearing a suit jacket right now, waving a AK47 in the air and yelling, "Wololololol" for no apparent reason. I realize that's a bit stereotypical but if your country condones burying women up to their necks and throwing rocks at their heads for reading, you deserve to cop a bit of flak. I'm sorry your government and infrastructure is a mess, and that you're at war because your invisible sky wizard says it's okay to eat goat testicles and someone else's invisible sky wizard says it's not, but yelling, "Wololololol" isn't going to fix anything. Sort it out, dickheads.

I realize 'sort it out, dickheads' isn't exactly groundbreaking foreign policy but honestly, if you've got time to stand around in rubble yelling, "Wolololololol", you've got time to sweep up a bit. The ones that ride around in the back of a pickup truck yelling, "Wolololololol" with fifteen other idiots aren't much better but at least they're going somewhere. Hopefully to Home Depot to buy a few brooms and construction strength garbage bags.

"Will that be all today?"
"Yes, just the brooms and construction strength garbage bags thank you. Oh, and this roll of Mentos. I haven't tried the green apple ones."
"Doing a bit of yard work this weekend?"
"Yes, I've got quite a bit of rubble to clean up. I tried standing on top of it and waving my gun about while yelling wolololololol but it didn't accomplish much."
"No? Well you have a nice day and death to America."
"Same to you. Allahu akbar."

When I was in fifth grade, our class had a guest speaker come in to talk to us about Papua New Guinean culture. He bought in a coconut and a machete and chopped the coconut in half to show us how sharp the blade was. He also showed us a documentary called *Mudmen of Papua New Guinea* about a tribe of natives that wear masks made out of mud. I had vivid nightmares for weeks afterwards about mudmen chasing me with machetes. I'll try drawing one of the masks so you can get an idea of how terrifying they were:

Right, well it didn't come out looking quite as terrifying as I remember. It looks more like a short ghost or a *South Park* character than a clay mask but you'll just have to imagine a black guy with a machete wearing it. He's chasing you through a shopping mall and your feet weigh a ton for some reason. Also, Emma Jenkins is at the shopping mall with John Stamos from *Full House* and they're holding hands.

The guest speaker also told us a story about a Papua New Guinean village leader named Mutengke. Apparently Mutengke had eight wives, which wasn't nearly enough for someone of his stature, so he sent an invitation to a neighboring village for prospective marriage candidates. The invitation stated that it was a great honor to be one of his wives, as his hut was large and waterproof, and that the candidates should arrive at noon the next day for consideration. It also stated that he was expecting a large turnout so candidates should bring their own mats to sit on.

Asking people to bring their own mats is probably the jungle equivalent of telling people to bring a chair to a barbecue. How good can a barbecue be if the host can't organize chairs? I'm not taking a chair anywhere. I'll stay at home with my vast selection of things to sit on if you can't get your act together.

"David, I'm having a barbecue tomorrow if you're free. I'll fire up the grill around noon."
"Do I have to bring anything?"
"No, just a chair."
"Are you having the barbecue in a field?"
"No, it's at my house but apparently we don't own any chairs. Oh, and it's BYO so bring something to drink and whatever you want put on the grill. And a side dish. Potato salad or something."
"So pack as if I'm going camping, got it. Will anything actually be provided?"
"The venue and great company."
"Right, I'll probably just stay home then."
"No, you have to come. I need you to pick up six bags of ice and a full propane bottle on the way. And a patio umbrella from Home Depot, it's going to be sunny.

I specifically tell people not to bring their own chairs when I have a barbecue. I paid a lot of money for our outdoor setting and I don't want anyone's shitty Coleman fold-up camping chairs ruining the layout. Not enough chairs? Stand. No, we're not bringing the dining room chairs outside, they're West Elm. Perhaps you shouldn't have invited your entire extended family of sixteen, Linda. One afternoon in your over-chlorinated pool honestly isn't worth this shit.

Noon came and went and nobody showed up for Mutengke's marriage auditions. Outraged by this blatant sign of disrespect, Mutengke sent a group of men to the neighboring village that night to hack their children to death with machetes. I raised my hand at this point in the story to ask the obvious question.

"Yes? The young man in the *Mork & Mindy* t-shirt?"
"Was it because of the mats?"
"Sorry?"
"The mats."
"I'm sorry, I don't understand what you're asking."
"The reason nobody showed up. Was it because Mutengke told them they had to bring their own mats?"
"No, the mats haven't got anything to with the story."
"It was on the invite. To bring mats."
"The mats don't matter."
"Then why didn't they go?"
"Because Mutengke was old and mean and their village was better. It was on a beach."
"Where was Mutengke's village?"
"In the jungle."
"You should have told us all that at the start of the story."
"David, shut up and let Mr Tonkwokoki finish."

A week after the massacre, Mutengke sent another invitation to the neighboring village and twelve women showed up. I assume with their own mats. You can probably tell where this is going.

The women were plump and of childbearing age so Mutengke decided he'd marry them all. To celebrate the upcoming marriages, the village held a feast that night which included copious amounts of tumbuna - a popular local alcoholic beverage made from fermented guava and taro roots.

Mutengke awoke the next morning to a silent village. The children and his prospective brides were gone, the adults had all had their throats cut in their sleep.

A week later, Mutengke, dirty and half-starved, wandered into the neighboring village. Apparently it was a better village that his. On a beach. Rather than being driven away, the villagers gave him a bowl of mumu - a traditional dish of pork and rice - and a mat to sit on at the edge of village.

For five days,* Mutengke watched the thriving village. The people were happy and sang and laughed as they went about their daily activities. He recognized two of his own children amongst the other children taken from his village and the twelve women he had planned to marry. The women played with the children, scolded them when they were naughty and consoled them when there were tears.

---

* *I assume he just sat on the mat the entire time. The story didn't cover this in detail but I've seen documentaries about tribes and there seems to be a lot of mat sitting. My favorite tribe is the African one that jumps.*

On the sixth day, one of the women bought Mutengke his daily bowl of mumu and he asked, "Why did you not kill me that night?"

The woman nodded towards a group of children playing nearby and asked, "Which of those children are yours?"

Mutengke pointed out his two sons.

"No," the woman corrected him, "Those children are ours. You have nothing. No people, no home. Even the mat you sit on does not belong to you. It was my daughters."

Mutengke lowered his head and stared into his bowl. The meat was tinged green. "This pork is rancid," he said.

"Yes," the woman replied, "It's two weeks old. And it's not pork."

Which is a bit rough. I think everyone in the class, including our teacher, was expecting a positive message, possibly even a happy ending such as Mutengke's sons taking him by the hand and saying, "Come over to the fire with the rest of the family, Father." But no, apparently keeping your enemies alive so you can feed them dead children was the message.

The class was silent for several seconds, then Mr Tonkwokoki yelled and waved about his machete. Several students screamed then giggled nervously, our teacher had a hearty guffaw and pantomimed having a heart attack. I thought it was odd and a bit of a cop out. The story didn't have an ending, just a jump-scare. Like the campfire story about the man with the white face and red eyes that looks in people's windows.

175

A few plot holes also stood out; firstly, if it was two weeks between when the children were slaughtered and Mutengke arrived at the village, why weren't the dead children already buried? Or did they dig a few back up when he got there? Secondly, why was Mutengke half-starved? Did the women take the village's food supply back with them? There wasn't a pig leg or a couple of coconuts left over from the feast the night before to tide Mutengke over? Also, who sleeps through everyone having their throats cut? I'm no expert but you'd think there'd be a bit of thrashing and gurgling going on and, after slaughtering a bunch of children with machetes, it would seem sensible to keep a few guards posted just in case the neighboring villagers also own machetes.

"Oh no, Mutengke's men have slaughtered our children. Should I tell everyone to grab their machetes?"

"No, give it a week and see if he sends another invitation. If he does, send the mothers of the dead children to steal their children and slaughter the adults while they sleep. Not Mutengke though, dead men feel no loss. Oh, and tell the women to bring back all the food."

"Right. Seems like an overly complicated plan but you're the boss. Should we bury our children in the meantime?"

"No, not yet."

I raised a couple of these plot holes with Mr Tonkwokoki but was told I'd missed the point of the story. Emma Jenkins asked if girls in Papua New Guinea wear grass skirts and was told it was an excellent question.

Horsepowers

I knew Holly wasn't going to understand. We'd agreed on a new Jeep as it was practical, reasonably fuel efficient, and capable in the snow.

It snows fairly often where we live. Not by Alaskan standards of course, but enough to need a vehicle that can make it up and down slippery roads between December and March. A few years back, it came almost to my crotch.

As we live in a rural area, without state-maintained roads, an old man named Doug clears the snow whenever he fucking feels like it or not at all. I guess he figures that if the forecast calls for snowfall all week, why not wait and do it all at once? I'm not exactly sure what our subdivision owners' fee covers - probably the fifty or so inflatable Christmas decorations he adds to his front yard around this time. It helps to think of the penguin inside a snowglobe and the waving snowman as our contribution to the neighborhood festivities. Nobody around here is caroling or swapping boiled puddings. We received a request from Doug a while back for an additional $250 to fix a pothole and it turned out it was in his driveway. I'm fairly sure that's not how it works but a conversation with Doug lasts around four hours so we just sent the cheque.

Before I knew better, when we hadn't been here more than a season, I had a two hour conversation with Doug on the street about a bear he once saw walk across his front lawn. Then he repeated the story as if he hadn't just told it. It wasn't a robot bear or a bear wearing pants. There was no wrestling or fending off with a sharp stick. A bear just walked across his lawn. A conversation regarding a bear walking across your lawn should consist of the fact, possibly a small amount of exaggeration for entertainment purposes, and maybe a sign-off such as, "So there you go," or, if you really need to retell the adventure, "So there you go, a bear walked across my lawn."

"I saw a bear walk across my front lawn once."
"Really?"
"Yes. A big one. So there you go, a bear walked across my lawn."

I just used the stopwatch on my phone to time how long it took to read that and, even allowing for a bit of nodding and pointing to get into character, it took just under twelve seconds. So there you go, my neighbour Doug once took two and a half hours to tell me that he saw a bear walk across his front lawn.

I did *sit* in the Jeep. I pressed a few switches and opened and closed the sunglasses holder. It's not as if I didn't look at it all. Holly and I had already done our research and it was the logical choice. I was there to buy a Jeep and it's entirely probable that if Holly hadn't had to work that day, if she'd been able to come with me to the dealer instead of hosting a stakeholder meeting for sad old men in stripey grey suits and their polyester clad fat wives, we'd have driven a Jeep off the lot.

"No trade-in?" Greg asked me. He was in his early fifties with a salt and pepper beard. There were three or four photos of children on his desk and one of him and a woman holding up a giant watermelon.

"Sorry?"
"No trade-in?"
"No, I'll keep the Kia for now. Sell it to a poor Mexican family or something. Are those your kids?"
"Yes, Daniel, Richard and Sarah. They're a bit older now. If you could sign here Mister Thorne... thank you, and here..."
"That's a pretty big watermelon."
"Hmm?"
"In the photo. Took you both to lift it did it?"
"Yes."
"Is that your wife?"
"Yes. Married thirty-five years."
"Good job. My wife will probably divorce me when I get home. Or kill me."
"Hahaha."
"I'm not joking. If I had to guess, I'd say a stabbing while I'm asleep or in the shower. Probably the shower because it'll

179

make less mess. You should talk me out of it."

"Talk you out of purchasing the vehicle?"

"Yes. Tell me it's a huge mistake and the engine is going to blow up or something."

"I'm not going to tell you that but we do have a large selection of other vehicles. The Jeep *is* an excellent option."

"Yes, but it's not... you know."

"Yes I do."

Greg had approached and introduced himself while I was sitting in the back of the Jeep. It's important to get Miss Daisy's point of view. He popped the bonnet and I nodded and pretended to know what I was looking at. I may have asked how many torques it had or something, just to appear knowledgeable. I strolled around a bit while I waited for him to return with the Jeep keys for a test drive. That's when I saw it. It was a few rows over, behind a selection of pickup trucks. It was white and sleek with a wide front grill. Reminiscent of the seventies but modern, mean, beautiful. My breath actually caught in my chest and my pulse rose.

Oh my god, I thought, I almost bought the Jeep. What if I hadn't seen it and bought the Jeep and then saw it as I was driving out in the Jeep? It would have been a cruel, devastating blow. Who knows how long it would have taken me to get over it. Probably never.

Greg returned to the Jeep, stood on tippy-toes looking around the lot for me. I waved and he made his way over.

"What the fuck is this?" I asked him.

"What the fuck is this?" asked Holly.
"It's a Dodge Challenger R/T 5.7 litre V8 Hemi."
"A what?"
"A Dodge Challenger R/T 5.7 litre V8 Hemi."
"What are you, twelve?"
"Don't make me take it back. I love it so much."
"What the fuck, David? What happened to the Jeep?"
"It was boring."
"So you bought a Hot Wheels car instead?"
"Look at it."
"I've seen them before. Rednecks drive them."
"Why would you say something like that when it's obviously
not true?"
"It is true. Ina's cousin Eustice owns one and he's as redneck
as they come. He lives in a trailer in the middle of a corn
field and thows axes."
"What at?"
"The axes? At a big bit of wood with a target on it. It's like
darts. But with axes."
"Oh my god, why haven't we got that? Is it an American
thing? Like beer hole or corn pong?"
"No, it's a redneck thing."
"I'm going to look it up on YouTube later."
"We agreed on a Jeep. I'm so disappointed right now I could
cry. I was going to drive it to work tomorrow."
"You can drive the Challenger to work."

"I work at a bank. In an office. Not on the streets racing Riddick for pink slips.

"Dominic."

"What?"

"He's Dominic Toretto in *The Fast and the Furious*. He's only Riddick in the space one. He's not Riddick in all of them."

"What are we going to do in the snow?"

"It has a low centre of gravity so one would assume it will do fairly well."

"Is it four wheel drive?"

"It might be. Who knows? Take it for a test drive."

After adjusting the rear and side mirrors, Holly put her seatbelt on and pushed the seat as far back as it could go. I'm a good five or six inches taller than Holly but whenever I get into a car she's driven, I can barely reach the steering wheel. I have no idea what's going on there but I have glanced over once or twice and caught her driving with her knees. I usually make a big production of getting the seat back to where I like it. This means stopping in the middle of the road several times after pulling out of the driveway as it's unsafe to adjust your seat position while driving.

Holly pressed the ignition button and the engine roared to life. A deep rumble, menacing and eager, promised danger and excitement.

"It's a bit loud," she said.

"It's meant to be. That's all the horsepowers."

She indicated and pulled out of our driveway, drove for a few miles while keeping the vehicle well below the speed limit. Turning onto a main road, Holly slowly accelerated up to the posted sixty miles per hour.

"It drives alright," she commented, giving a little nod of approval.
"We may as well have taken the Kia for a spin. Give it a bit of petrol."
"I'm doing sixty."
"It's not a car for doing sixty in if the speed is posted as sixty, it's a badass car for badasses who play by their own rules. Take it up to sixty-four."
"I'm happy at sixty. Can you put the radio on NPR, please?"
"Oh my god, Holly. We should be listening to *Ribbons* by The Sister's of Mercy or Linkin Park's *I'll Be Gone*, not to lesbians discussing climate change and glass ceilings."
"You have a very narrow point of view about things sometimes. I enjoy listening to NPR. It's informative. What the fuck is this old lady doing?"

A Nissan Cube pulled out in front of us and Holly slowed to accommodate, keeping the three-second rule of distance between both vehicles. We tore along the highway at forty-five, listening to some guy who called in to a show about puppets to argue that Gerry Anderson deserves far more recognition than Jim Henson for his contribution to the marionette-based arts.

"Just pull around her."

"I will when I have a safe spot to pass."

"You can see two miles ahead of us. Nobody's coming."

"Fine."

Holly indicated, checked, and pulled out to pass. She pressed the accelerator. Hard.

Our other car, a Kia, needs the accelerator slammed to move away from traffic lights and overtaking is something other people do. Seb and I timed the Kia once to see how long it took to get up to sixty and we both lost interest well before. We were on our way to Lowe's to purchase a stack of bricks to construct a firepit at the time. After loading up the Kia, we had to stick a leg out and push Flintstone style just to get moving. As there's a decent sized hill before our house, we had to unload the bricks at the bottom and drive them up in small batches. The Kia is insured so I park it under a large dead tree during extreme wind warnings.

Fuel and air ignited. The engine howled.

Holly let a small yelp of surprise as the wheels spun, gripped, threw the vehicle forward. I let out a larger yelp as I was thrown back in my seat. We tore past the Nissan Cube like it was travelling backwards. With a glance in the rear mirror, Holly eased back on the accelerator and back into our lane. I glanced at the speedometer, watched it drop from well over a hundred to ninety, then eighty. Holly sat on eighty.

"Its got pretty good pickup," Holly shouted. She sounded odd. "How many horsepowers does it actually have?"

"I don't know, I'm not a mechanic. It's a V8 so at least eight. You should probably slow down a little bit."

"I'm not going *that* fast."

"Yes you are. It just seems slow after coming out of warp speed. At least take it down to seventy."

Holly slowed down to seventy to take a soft corner, powered out of it doing ninety.

"Seriously, you're going to get a speeding ticket," I advised, "there's police along this road all the time."

"I could probably outrun them."

"Who are you? If a deer jumps out in the middle of the road right now, it will go straight through the windshield and kick me to death."

"Fine."

"Thank you."

"You can change the radio station if you like. Put on something with a bit of bass."

"No, NPR is fine. I'm kind of interested now. Who knew Indonesia had such a rich history of puppetry?"

"I need cigarettes. Do you want a coffee?"

"Not from Sheetz."

For those unfamiliar with Sheetz, it's a service station - or gas station - in America, with a mini supermarket and hot food. They make terrible coffee and everyone that works there hates their life and you. In Australia, service stations are commonly referred to as 'the servo'. Diminutive forms of words are commonly used in everyday Australian English. Blowflies are blowies, tracksuit pants are tracky dacks, sunglasses are sunnies. It isn't cute or 'oh so Australian', it stems from laziness and anger at having to use more than one syllable. Whole sentences are often replaced with a single diminutive, or grunt, and a conversation that might normally consist of, "I'm just going to go for a drive to the service station as I'm out of cigarettes, I'll be back shortly," becomes a shake of the keys and, "Servo. Ciggies."

Holly only ever buys one packet of cigarettes. She's been giving up' for almost three years now but likes to keep up the pretence of it being her last pack. I've never had the slightest inclination to stop smoking but I can't image it would be all that hard if I wanted to. Wanting to is the only reason I do anything really. There's things I do that I don't want to do, like work, but that's only because I want to buy things more than I want to not work. I want to enjoy that first taste of smooth smoke with my morning coffee much more than I can ever imagine wanting to run a marathon. I assume that's the same way fat women feel about cake and good on them I say. Nobody wants to see them running anyway.

Holly turned off the ignition and stated she'd back shortly. I lent my elbow out of the window, watched as a guy held the entrance door open for her. He had a big bushy beard like a lumberjack and I know Holly has a thing for lumberjacks. He smiled and said, "Nice car."

"Thanks," Holly replied, "it's a V8."

Arriving home last week, by drifting the length of the driveway and performing a handbrake stop, Holly called me out to admire her new twenty-inch rims. I don't get to drive the Challenger much. Holly drives it to work everyday so I generally just use the Kia. It's practical and fuel efficient. This morning, Holly told me she wants a Mopar cold air intake system for Christmas.

Costco

"Seb, try one of these samples."
"Why?"
"They're free."
"So?"
"Free is always good."
"Not if it's a free snake."

Photography

I blame Melissa. She was the one who said, "I know someone" when the photographer we usually use was unavailable and his backup indisposed. Afterwards she stated, "Well I don't *know him, know him*, he took the photos at my sister's wedding. They weren't all that good though."

From: David Thorne
Date: Wednesday 14 October 2015 10.55am
To: Robert Lawson
Subject: Patio photos

Hello Robert,

We received the flash drives this morning, thank you for couriering them to us so quickly.

I had Jodie copy the images over and we are both a little confused. Are these placeholder images? If so, when can we expect final photos?

In order to meet deadline, we require final photos by this Friday to have client approval before next Tuesday when the printers are expecting artwork.

Regards, David.

From: Robert Lawson
Date: Wednesday 14 October 2015 11.19am
To: David Thorne
Subject: Re: Patio photos

They are the final photos.

Rob

....

From: David Thorne
Date: Wednesday 14 October 2015 11.33am
To: Robert Lawson
Subject: Re: Re: Patio photos

Hello Robert,

Thank you for getting back to me so quickly. I've checked the proposal and it states the $3200 covers the "commission and delivery of professionally staged photographs."

The brief called for photos of a family enjoying year-round use of their patio - barbecuing, having a party, that kind of thing. The promotional material we are designing for the client is intended to be aspirational.

Twenty-eight snapshots of an overweight woman sitting in a chair provides little aspiration. Unless it's to have diabetes and what appears to be deep vein thrombosis.

Regards, David

From: Robert Lawson
Date: Wednesday 14 October 2015 11.58am
To: David Thorne
Subject: Re: Re: Re: Patio photos

Those are the only photos I could get. The photos were taken on a new Nikon D5500 which is 24.2 megapixel. You can't get any higher resolution than that.

Rob

....

From: David Thorne
Date: Wednesday 14 October 2015 12.17pm
To: Robert Lawson
Subject: Re: Re: Re: Re: Patio photos

Robert,

I'm not questioning the resolution. Being able to zoom in on an image while retaining sharp detail is hardly a bonus in this instance though. The model chosen looks like she is waiting at a bus stop on her way to spend Kohl's Cash. Probably on another pair of brown slacks.

Which photo would you suggest for the cover? The one of her raising her thumb or the one of her holding a slice of cantaloupe? Of the twenty-six remaining photos, seventeen show her sitting cross legged pointing at things and the other nine are blurry.

It was indicated in the first meeting that the price for photography included talent and props for the day, i.e. four adults, three children, cake and sparklers, food and wine. I don't recall 'grabbing Nan and sticking her outside by herself with a slice of cantaloupe' being discussed as a possible alternative.

What exactly did the $3200 cover?

Regards, David

....

From: Robert Lawson
Date: Wednesday 14 October 2015 12.41pm
To: David Thorne
Subject: Re: Re: Re: Re: Re: Patio photos

The $3200 covered camera equipment and my time. I took the photos and I don't appreciate you insulting my wife. People who are in their fifties build patios and most people just relax on their patios not have parties. It's about the patio.

The other people I asked to be there on the day had to take their dog to the vet to be put down and I didn't have time to organize anyone else.

If you want me to take more photos I can but I won't be able to get them to you before Friday.

Rob

From: David Thorne
Date: Wednesday 14 October 2015 1.12pm
To: Robert Lawson
Subject: Re: Re: Re: Re: Re: Re: Patio photos

Hello Robert,

Thank you for the offer but we won't be requiring more photographs of your wife - with or without additional sad family members.

We will, however, keep you in mind should we ever find ourselves commissioned to design brochures titled *Locating Backyard Items* or *Healthy Alfresco Snacks for the Lonely*.

As the $3200 agreed to was for the commission and delivery of professionally staged photographs, not to 'buy Robert a nice camera', I have notified the accounts department that we will not be paying that portion of your invoice.

We have, however, agreed to pay your $280 charge for 'burning' twenty-eight images to twenty-eight 128MB flash drives. Mainly because nobody knew quite how to react to the situation and Kevin in accounting said he can use the drives to send electronic Christmas cards to his friends and relatives this year.

Regards, David

From: Robert Lawson
Date: Wednesday 14 October 2015 1.26pm
To: David Thorne
Subject: Re: Re: Re: Re: Re: Re: Re: Patio photos

You have to pay the invoice in full for the amount agreed on. I'm out $2900 on the camera equipment alone plus travel and meetings.

You don't just get to say whether you pay or not after I've done the work. What planet do you live on?

Rob

....

From: David Thorne
Date: Wednesday 14 October 2015 1.52pm
To: Robert Lawson
Subject: Re: Re: Re: Re: Re: Re: Re: Re: Patio photos

Hello Robert,

You were present during the meeting in which we discussed project requirements.

At no point during that meeting did you put your hand up and ask, "How set on the whole 'family enjoying the benefits of year-round outdoor living' thing are you? I had more of a 'tuck-shop lady giving directions and handling fruit' approach in mind."

The fact that your fee covered the purchase price of equipment to fulfill the commission isn't reason to pay that fee but it does explain a lot. Is this your first camera?

Based on your business model, I'm considering opening my own surgery. I have no formal training in the field of medicine but if I order a stack of business cards with 'David Thorne, Professional Surgeon' printed on them and charge my first patient for a set of robes and a decent scalpel, I should be good to go. If questioned over fees after being admitted for an appendectomy and leaving with a pamphlet on toe fungus, I'll simply explain to them the 'out of pocket system' of business startup.

We have arranged for a capable photographer to redo the shoot on short notice. Project costs allocated to the commission and delivery of professionally staged photographs are therefore covered.

We will not be paying your invoice, recommending you to anyone, or listening to Melissa ever again when she says she "knows someone."

Regards, David

From: Robert Lawson
Date: Wednesday 14 October 2015 2.18pm
To: David Thorne
Subject: Re: Re: Re: Re: Re: Re: Re: Re: Re: Patio photos

If I haven't received full payment within 14 days, I'll be taking legal action.

Rob

....

From: David Thorne
Date: Wednesday 14 October 2015 2.29pm
To: Robert Lawson
Subject: Re: Re: Re: Re: Re: Re: Re: Re: Re: Re: Patio photos

Hello Robert,

If you need someone to represent you, let me know. I have a friend who could do with the cash. He makes very little as a Sandwich Artist so I'm sure if he can organise a briefcase and get someone to take his shift, he'd be happy to show up on the day and give it a whack.

Regards, David

From: Robert Lawson
Date: Wednesday 14 October 2015 3.04pm
To: David Thorne
Subject: Re: Re: Re: Re: Re: Re: Re: Re: Re: Re: Re: Patio photos

See you in court.

Scrabble

"David."

"Nnnnn?"

"Are you awake?"

"What?"

"Are you awake?"

"No."

"I had a bad dream."

"Okay."

"There were zombies everywhere and we had to leave the house and we were really tired because we had to climb a hill but the zombies didn't get tired, they just kept coming."

"There's no such thing as zombies. Go back to sleep."

"That's when they get you. When you sleep."

"Right, we'll take turns on watch then. I'll sleep now while you keep lookout and we'll switch in a few hours."

"At the top of the hill there was a farmhouse owned by an old lady who grew her own vegetables. We stayed there and you built a big fence to keep the zombies out."

"She just let us live there?"

"She was nice. And it was a big farmhouse with lots of rooms."

"So the old lady gets a new fence and we live rent-free on a self-sustainable farm? That sounds like a pretty good arrangement to me."

"Well it wasn't 'pretty good' because the zombies easily got through the fence. You should have made it stronger. You say you know how to make things but they come out terrible and everyone dies."

"Nice."

"It's like the coffee table. You should have watched a YouTube video or something before making it. It's all wobbly. If you put a cup of tea on it and someone bumps the edge, the tea spills everywhere. It doesn't even have to be a big bump. We should just take it outside and burn it."

"I didn't make that. We bought it from IKEA."

"You put it together."

"Fine, if we are ever living in an old lady's farmhouse on the top of a hill during a zombie apocalypse and I need to build a fence, I'll watch a YouTube instructional video prior to construction."

"It'll be too late then, there won't be any Internet. It will be down. Everything will be down. You'd need look up how to build a fence well in advance."

"Holly, it's... 3.40am. I'm going back to sleep. Why don't *you* look it up and if I ever need to construct a zombie-proof fence, you can supervise."

"What if I'm already dead?"

"Then I'll be dead too. I'll go down protecting you."

"You're just saying that. In my dream, you made it to the top of the hill a lot quicker than I did."

"We both know that's not really possible. You jog every morning and go to the gym three times a week. I get winded making toast."

"You discover untapped strength when you're being chased by zombies. Like that lady who managed to lift an entire tree when her baby was trapped under it."

"What was the baby doing under a tree?"

"I don't know, I think the tree fell down in a storm."

"Why was the lady outside during a storm with her baby and why wasn't she trapped as well? Did she throw the baby and run when she saw the tree falling? The entire story is full of holes and probably completely fabricated. Or, at best, largely exaggerated. It might have been a twig or small branch and, through retellings like your own, became an example of found strength during need."

"No, it was a big tree. An oak or something. Scientists measured it afterwards and it was ten feet thick."

"Ten feet? That *is* a big tree. If it is a true story, and I fully accept it may be now that scientists are involved, she would have needed to construct some kind of pulley system or at least use a lever and fulcrum."

"Fine, if we are ever being chased by zombies, I'll use adrenaline to get away and you can fuck around with a long stick and a triangle. Then it will just me and the old lady and her son living in the farmhouse."

"You didn't mention the old lady had a son."

"No, because I knew you'd be jealous."

"I'm not jealous, I'm just wondering why the son didn't help with the fence. Living on a farm, I'm sure he's built fences before. How old was he?"

"I don't know, late twenties."

"Well, there you go. Was he strapping?"

"See."

"No, I'm just trying to get a clearer picture of what's going on. I'm outside building a fence, the old lady is probably tending to her veggies, and you and Cletus are doing what? It's beginning to sound less like a zombie apocalypse than a Mills & Boon novel."

"His name wasn't Cletus, it was Roger."

"Really? What were you and Roger up to while everyone else was doing chores?"

"Nothing."

"Hmm. Well, I'm killing Roger. And his mom. Fuck them, it means more veggies for us. "

"You can't just kill the people who save us and give us shelter."

"Call the police, I don't give a fuck. It's their own fault for being so trusting. I'm killing them both. Then it will just be us and Samantha."

"Who's Samantha?"

"The old lady's twenty-four-year-old daughter."

"There's no daughter."

"Yes there is. She's Roger's much better looking sister."

"Well I'm killing her too. If anyone asks, we'll just say zombies got them."

"That works. It's good to have a plan for this type of thing. Can I go back to sleep now?"

"We should get them to help with the fence first. And show us around so we know how everything works."

"Yes, it would be good to know the Netflix password and where they keep the extra towels."

"Netflix would be down. But we could play Scrabble. We haven't played Scrabble in ages."

"I hate Scrabble."

"Roger liked Scrabble."

Gypsies

"Oh my god, you are terrible at this game," Seb stated, "it's like playing with a two-year-old. Why are you standing in the corner spinning?"

"It's the controller," I replied, "I'm not used to using a controller, I need a keyboard and mouse. Like in *Quake*. Remember *Quake*?"

"Yes."

"You looked around with the mouse and moved with the arrow keys. If you saw the other player, you clicked the mouse button to send a rocket in their direction. They'd explode if you hit them. First one not to explode ten times won. That's it. There wasn't forty-eight different things to remember. How did you know I'm in a corner?"

"I'm looking right at you. Just follow me out of the building."

"Okay, but don't kill me. Where are you?"

"Oh my god, I'm standing right next to you on the ledge. Look up, see? I'm jumping."

"How do I look up?"

"Oh my god, use the other stick."

"Oh right..."

"What did you kill me for?"

"Sorry, it was an accident. I pressed the wrong button."

"Bullshit." Seventeen thousand miles away in Australia, Seb exited the game.

I used to be able to beat Seb at all the games we played. *Quake, Unreal Tournament, Need for Speed Most Wanted.* Then he hit puberty. And I left him. For work, for love, for sanity, for a dozen reasons logical and not. Moving countries meant the opportunity for Seb to travel though, to spend quality time together rather than every second weekend and a few nights between at my small apartment - Seb's mother and I never saw eye to eye about much. It also meant stretches where I wouldn't see him at all, where I would worry and miss out on things and long to hear his voice.

The thought of him being seventeen thousand miles away was pushed back daily. Sometimes I couldn't push it back and I would spend days, weeks, angry and depressed. We'd message and Facetime and play games online but every time I met him at the airport he was taller. This year he was taller than me.

He's also better looking than I was at sixteen. Smarter and funnier. Or, perhaps all parents just think their offspring are smart and attractive. It's possible he may be retarded and have a face like a smashed crab but I simply can't see it. I thought he might be gay for a while, assumed actually, but I've seen his Internet history since. I should probably talk to him about that, ask him for a list of good links or something. Apart from basic biology, I never had 'the' talk with Seb. I never filtered his Internet search settings either though. I figured he'd work it out. There was no Internet when I was his age. I'd never heard of rimjobs or creampies or pancakes.

What I knew came from secondhand exaggerations and my father's hidden magazine collection. My very first love and loss was Miss Penthouse 1980, she liked campfires and hiking. I lost her when the carefully removed centrefold went through the washing machine in the back pocket of my jeans. I'm lucky my mother didn't check the pockets or I'd not even have had the mushy folded lump to remember her by. I kept the lump for a while, tried to dry it out, you could still make out one of her ears and a bit of the mosquito netting.

My second love and loss was a woman named Natalie, I was Seb's age. She was forty-something and worked as a gardener for the Tea Tree Gully Golf Club. She told me I looked like Simon Le Bon. I don't know if Seb has had sex yet. If he has, I hope it wasn't behind a hedge. Perhaps he's too busy playing *The Modern Black Ops*.

My third love and loss slept with a furniture delivery man when Seb was four. I won't go into that except to say the delivery man's name was Stuart and he liked the band Cold Chisel. They dated for a while after I left but she's had eighty or ninety boyfriends since then. Before our paths diverged, Seb had regime, a set bedtime, healthy food triangles.*

---

*Adding shelves doesn't make it a pyramid.

After becoming a part-time father, I didn't want the limited time he was with me further limited by rules. There were no healthy food triangles, we ate McDonald's and pizza. There was no set bedtime as I didn't want him to go to bed. Sleeping was time he wasn't spending with me. There were no regimes at all. I realise it's not an award-winning parental model but at least I never molested or beat him. I did threaten to sell him to the Gypsies on occasion, and once to send him to boarding school, but they weren't actual options.

"What's a Gypsie?"

"People that travel around the country in caravans."

"Like Nana?"

"No, Nana has a house. She travels around the country in a caravan for fun. Gypsies don't have houses. They live in the caravan full-time, travelling from town to town, buying children apparently."

"What do they do with them?"

"I have no idea, probably sell them on at a profit."

"How much would they pay you?"

"For you? Not much. There's not a huge market for kids who draw shit on the walls with a Sharpie. What's it meant to be anyway? Is it a penis?"

"No, it's an arrow."

"You should have made it more pointy then. Why did you draw a giant arrow on the wall?"

"So people know the way to my room."

"Right, because we get a lot of people wandering about lost, wondering where the fuck your bedroom is. At least when the Gypsies come I can tell them, 'Yes, he's in his room, straight through and down the hall, just follow the huge fucking arrow.' Do it again and I'll send you to boarding school."

"What's boarding school?"

"Same as normal school but you get molested and beaten. Then they sell you to the Gypsies. We get half each."

There were days when I had to work. Lots of days really. Days when I had to meet deadlines, days he came to client meetings, days he sat in front of the Playstation. He survived. We went away a few times a year, camping and houseboating mostly, but more hours than not were spent inside a small concrete box. Between client changes and emails, we played *War of the Monsters* and *Ratchet & Clank*, *Unreal Tournament* and *Quake*.

I spotted him easily amongst the crowd of tired faces pouring through the exit. A full head height taller than most, his designer haircut added another four or five inches. He grinned, slid his bag across the polished tiles towards me. I hugged him hard.

"Are you shrinking?" he asked.

"It's these shoes," I replied, "they have thin soles."

"My soles are thin too."

"Not as thin as these, I can't even walk on gravel with them. How was the flight?"

"Long. Fifteen hours long."

When Seb was six, he walked to the corner shop by himself for the first time. It was December of 2005 and he was with me for a full week of the holidays. I'd bought him a mini-bike for Christmas on the Internet. It wasn't a brand name like Yamaha or Honda, it was a Chinese knockoff called Zoomyou, or something like that, and I think it was made of cast iron. It was delivered the week before Christmas and I hid it in the garage under a sheet. Our concrete box, identical to twenty other concrete boxes in the Cul-de-sac, consisted of three stories with the living areas above the garage and bedrooms at the top.

Around 2am Christmas morning, I climbed out of bed and checked on Seb. He was snoring. I closed his book, turned off his bedlight, and shut his door quietly. Making my way down two flights, I uncovered the mini-bike and rolled it to the doorway leading upstairs. My intention was to carry it up to the living area so that when he awoke in the morning, he'd discover it besides the Christmas tree. I bent over, and lifted.

It felt like someone had tazed me, frying every nerve from my tailbone to my eye-sockets. I dropped to my knees, unable to move. I'd never experienced a thrown back before. Afterwards, just sneezing or getting a teaspoon out of the dishwasher was enough to throw it out but before that moment, back problems were 'old people' problems. The doorway was blocked by the bike and even if it hadn't been, I wouldn't have made it up the stairs. Every movement, every slight twist, produced white flashes of pain. I called out for Seb but knew it was pointless, he was two levels above with his bedroom door closed. With my knees and head on the concrete, doggy style, I waited.

Seb awoke and ran down to the second level excitedly. There were no presents under the tree and I wasn't anywhere in the house. He sat on the couch and cried. I heard the sobs, tried to time my calls for help between. Eventually he investigated.

After doting over the mini-bike, he fetched painkillers from the upstairs bathroom cabinet and, after a time, I was able to inch up the steps on my hands and knees. With help I made it into a leather office chairs on wheels. From there, I watched him climb up on the kitchen counter to reach the cupboard where his other presents were hidden, watched him make me a coffee for the first time, prepare his own breakfast.

Christmas in Australia is in the middle of summer and it's a common tradition to spend the day at the beach. Some people set up tables with prepared dishes, some eat fish 'n' chips cross legged on the sand. Seb and I didn't go to the beach. We didn't visit family or friends. We played *Need For Speed* and had pizza delivered.

It was the first time Seb ever answered the door and paid for the pizza by himself. For five days, he wheeled me from in front of the television to the bathroom and back. He made snacks, took the rubbish out, vacuumed the rugs and walked to the corner shop to buy milk for my coffees.

Seb tried out his mini-bike a few weeks later at a grassy picnic area beside a river. He forgot where the brakes were and 'bailed out' at speed by jumping off the back. The bike kept going, cleared the river bank by at least fifteen feet, and disappeared below the murky brown surface with barely a splash. Seb and I stood on the bank, watching as a few smokey bubbles broke the surface. "Lucky I jumped off," he said.

"You can sleep in the car on the drive home if you'd like."
"No, I slept a few hours on the plane. I wouldn't mind stopping at a Starbucks on the way though."
"We can do that. Do you want to drive?"
"I don't have my license yet."
"After we get out of the carpark then. Just be careful near rivers."
"Hmm."
"Because you might drive into them."
"Yes, I get it. It just wasn't very funny."
"Yes it was."
"Fine, for the next six weeks, I'm going to say, "Remember to lift with your knees" every time you pick up something."
"Hmm."
"You know, because you hurt your back ten years ago."
"Yes, I get it. There's no way you'd be able to keep it up for more than a few days though."

He managed to keep it up for almost a week. It was annoying after the first hour. It's actually surprising how many times during a day you pick things up. I ended up wearing cargo pants just so I could keep things in my pockets.

"Remember to lift with your knees."
"You can't say it after asking me to pass you something. That's entrapment. There needs to be rules. "
"Picking up something is picking up something."
"Right, well no then, I won't pass you the fucking remote control. It's going in the fourth pocket down, left leg, with the brass hose fitting and ATV keys."
"Oh my god, you don't have to say where you are putting things every time."
"It's an aide-mémoire. Ask me where something is."
"Where's Zambia?"
"Something that's in my pockets."
"Fine. Where are your reading glasses?"
"Second pocket down, right leg, with your laser pointer, a Snicker's bar, and six lighters."
"It's not exactly a special talent, is it?
"No, not really. "
"Can I have the ATV keys, please?"

The ATV had been delivered two weeks early. It was meant to come the day before Christmas. I was pretty annoyed at this as it meant having to get Seb another present for Christmas morning. You can't have everyone opening their presents and carrying on while one person watches television or scrolls 9Gag. He had a sock with his name on it hanging over the fireplace but it only had a packet of raisins and two used glow-sticks in it.

"Look Seb, Holly got me a patio heater. That'll come in handy."
"Huh, yeah."
"You're not eating your raisins?"

The ATV purchase made sense. Our property has a few acres of wooded land with creeks and a river nearby. It backs onto the George Washington National Forest. There's a fat lady who lives in our area that rides her ATV everywhere. I've seen her at the supermarket, the bank, and going through McDonald's drive-thru. I sat behind her doing 25mph on a single lane road for ten minutes once. She was eating an icecream. Another time, she sat at the traffic lights in front of me with a police car in front of her. She waved to them and they waved back. I have no idea what's going on, it's as if the law simply doesn't apply to her. She has no indicators. I'm pretty sure that if I rode an ATV to the supermarket even once, I'd be pulled over and told to stop being a dickhead.

"You're going to go for a ride now? I thought we were going to TJ-Maxx to buy you thick socks?"
"I can just wear two or three socks over each other. It's the same thing. I'd rather finish the ATV trail."
"Alright. Maybe Santa will bring you thick socks."

By anyone's standards our trail was pretty pitiful. It was steep in places, dangerously steep in others. Sides of hills had been dug into with a shovel and pickaxe just enough to allow crossing on slightly less than a forty-five degree angle. Leaning was essentially the key to not rolling. We'd built a small bridge over a creek but it was less scary to ride around it. The trail ended abruptly at the top of a hill where you had to make a five point turn and head back the way you came. To extend the trail further, along a ridge and back down to where it could loop back on itself, we needed to remove a pine tree blocking the way. Seb attached the chainsaw to the front of the ATV with straps, hopped on, and revved the engine. He patted the seat behind him.

"Why do I have to be on the back?"

"Just get on."

"You go too fast, let me go on the front."

"I won't go too fast. I promise."

"I'm not fucking around, Seb. If you go too fast I'll never trust you again. I get that it's hilarious to slide around corners and take jumps at speed but I know a guy who broke his neck mucking about on an ATV."

"Who do you know that broke their neck?"

"Just a guy I know."

"What's his name then?"

"... Bradley."

"Bradley what?"

"Cooper."

"The actor?"

"No, a different Bradley Cooper. Brad Cooper. He's an accountant. He was riding on the back of an ATV and the guy driving flipped it on a bend."

"Who was driving?"

"Just another guy."

"What was his name?"

"...Daniel."

"Daniel what?"

"Radcliffe."

"The guy who played Harry Potter?"

"Goddamit."

"Just get on."

"Fine."

I'd never cut a tree down before. I've seen people doing it on television but it is an entirely different matter when you are standing at the base looking up. I vaguely recalled an Alaskan bushman cutting a V shape but I couldn't remember if that meant the tree would fall with the V or away from it. The initial plan of 'just cutting it down and stepping away from the direction it falls' turned into 'cutting into it a little bit and running away in case it falls'. We repeated the process a dozen times until less than an inch of wood remained. Neither of us wanted to be standing under the pine when it fell, especially with a running chainsaw, so we tried pushing it. It wouldn't budge.

"How is it even possible that it's still standing?" I asked, "it's against all physics."

"Just cut it the rest of the way through. It'll be fine."

"Why don't *you* cut it then? It's probably not as big a deal as we are making out to be, we've just fed each other's apprehension until it turned into one."

"I'm not cutting it."

"What we need is a good strong breeze."

"We could try tying a rope around it and pulling it over with the ATV," suggested Seb.

"Then it would definitely fall on us. Besides, we don't have rope."

"We could use the garden hose. It's a hundred feet and the tree is probably only eighty."

"That's actually a pretty good idea."

It wasn't a pretty good idea. It was an ill-conceived and dangerous one. Seb rode back and collected the hose. He had a can of Coke and a packet of chips while he was back at the house which I thought was a bit rude. I sat on a log until I heard him returning, then pretended I had been digging rocks out of the path the whole time. We wrapped one end of the hose around the pine and tied a knot, the other to the back of the ATV. Seb rode down the path until the hose was taut, I stood further back and gave him the thumbs up. He revved the engine and moved forward. The pine swayed and creaked but held, rocking back and forth as he released the throttle.

"Try it again," I yelled, "if you can get it to rock, it should snap."

Seb rode forward faster this time, reversed, rode forward again. The tree rocked towards us, rocked back and cracked. The idea had gone better than expected; with the tree falling away from us, we wouldn't have to cut it up and remove it from the path, it would simply roll down the other side of the hill towards the river.

During warmer months, we sometimes jump from the rocky banks of the river - swimming back quickly before whatever's beneath the brown murky surface tries to eat us. I touched the bottom with my foot once so I always do a kind of 'safety jump' now where you spread out your arms and legs like a jumping jack. It's not quite as elegant as a cannonball but I don't like my head going under the water. We watched a dead cow float past once.

The tree hit the ground with a crash, bounced a bit, then started to roll. Seb looked at me in panic as the ATV was pulled backwards, his mouth and eyes wide like that painting of the bald guy on a bridge. He gripped the brake lever hard. The large knobbly tread of the wheels fought against the pull for a moment, stretching the hose as far as it could before losing traction in the dirt. Credit where credit's due, Briggs & Stratton make pretty strong hoses.

"Squeeze the brakes!" I yelled as I chased after him carefully. There are snakes in the forest so I had to watch where I was putting my feet. I realise this could be construed as a priority conflict but, you know, snakes.

"I *am* squeezing the brakes!" Seb screamed as the ATV disappeared over the summit and headed down.

"Don't you dare jump off!"

The pine reached the bank and hit a boulder. It bounced over and dropped four or five feet into the river below. Ninety-odd feet up the hill, the ATV was jerked hard. Despite being told otherwise, Seb was in mid-process of jumping off when the shunt pulled the handlebars into his waist. His arms and torso were thrown across the front of the ATV, his legs kicked the air. I watched him fumble for grip, looking up at me in horror as the ATV hit the bank and sailed over. It was exactly like that scene in Cliffhanger except on an ATV and without any mountain climbing equipment or holding hands.

At a brisk jog, it took me about ten seconds to reach the edge and look over. Seb was standing chest deep in water looking back up at me.

"Are you alright?" I asked, equally relieved and shocked he wasn't dead.

"No, I'm wet."

"Are you hurt?"

"No."

"How the fuck are you not hurt? You just went over a cliff backwards into a river. Where's the ATV?"

"I'm standing on it."

Seb felt around with his foot until he located the hose and pulled it up. There was plenty of slack between it and the pine which had drifted and turned in the current, wedging itself between banks fifty feet downstream. There was no possible way of getting the ATV back up where it had gone in so Seb swam and waded to the opposite bank. I met him there by walking gingerly across the pine. It rolled a bit when I was almost to the other side but luckily the water was only a few feet deep at that point.

"Jesus, that's cold. Look, I'm soaked to my knees."

"Are you joking? I went all the way in. I had to swim across while holding the hose."

"If you'd held the brakes for a few seconds longer instead of deciding to ditch, neither of us would be wet. You're wetness is due to your decision. My wetness is also due to your decision, not one of my own, therefore my wetness level, regardless of it being a lesser wetness level than yours, warrants a greater degree of concern."

"Can you stop saying wetness please? Besides, you're only wet because you can't balance on a log."

"Crossing the log wouldn't have been necessary if you hadn't ditched. Really, you owe me an apology. And a new pair of shoes. I've only had these a month and really liked them. The soles are a bit thin but they are pretty comfy otherwise. You can't just dry out wet leather shoes, they stretch and are never the same."

"I could have died."

"Not everything has to be about you, Seb."

With our arms wrapped around the hose, our heels deep in the soft pebbly bank, we pulled the ATV across the bottom of the river. It caught on hidden rocks and branches a few times but Seb waded in and wrestled it loose. He managed a kind of sobbing cheer when the handlebars finally broke the surface, another as the seat appeared.

"One more good pull," Seb declared, "On three okay? One, two..."
"Ngghhhh!"

I waited on all fours, doggystyle, almost an hour for Seb to return with the bottle of painkillers. He'd had a hot shower and changed while back at the house which is a whole new level of rude. I told him I was going to check if the Gypsies have an age limit.

Despite having been fully submerged, the ATV started on the third or fourth try so I'll certainly buy Honda products again. I haven't received any form of compensation for mentioning Honda's quality products, that have a positive impact on all our lives, so you can trust me when I say Honda believe the Power of Dreams® is realized when we work together to make them real.

As we were on the opposite side of the river, Seb had to ride through a farmer's paddock and along a main road for a couple of miles or so before he could cut through to our property. Apparently he passed a police car on his way and they waved. I mentioned this to the officer a few weeks later when I was pulled over for riding the ATV less than four hundred feet to our subdivision's mailboxes, but he still gave me a ticket and made me push the ATV home.

"It's snowing again," said Seb, "do you want me to pause the game and push you to the window so you can see?"
"I can see it from here. Sorry we can't go snowboarding like we planned."
"That's okay."
Did you like your presents? Are your socks warm?"
"Yeah, they're pretty good. Where are you?"
"I'm inside the abandoned mall. Meet me at the escalators. I promise I won't shoot you. Do you want to know what Holly's parents got you?"
"No, I can wait until she gets back."
"A Transformers shower curtain for your bathroom."
"Are you serious?"
"Yes. They got me a towel with a space shuttle on it."
"How do you know?"
"Holly's terrible at keeping secrets. I knew you got me the keyboard and mouse two weeks ago. You could have gone with her for Christmas lunch you know. Her dad makes a pretty decent dryball."
"I'm good with pizza... oh my god, Dad!"
"It was an accident, I pressed the wrong button."
"Bullshit."

About the Author

David Thorne, born 20 December 1946, is an Israeli illusionist, television personality, and psychic. He is known for his trademark television performances of spoon bending. His career as an entertainer has spanned more than four decades, with television shows and appearances in many countries.

Thorne was born in Tel Aviv, which was at that time part of the British Mandate of Palestine, to Jewish parents from Hungary and Austria.

At the age of eleven, Thorne's family moved to Nicosia, Cyprus, where he attended a high school, the Terra Santa College, and learned English. At the age of eighteen, he served in the Israeli Army's Paratroopers Brigade and was wounded in action during the 1967 Six-Day War. He worked as a photographic model in the late sixties and, during that time, began to perform for small audiences as a nightclub entertainer.

Thorne first started to perform in theatres, public halls, auditoriums, military bases and universities in Israel.

By the mid-seventies, he had become known in the United States and Europe. He also received attention from the scientific community, whose members were interested in examining his reported psychic abilities. A study by Stanford Research Institute (now known as SRI International), conducted by parapsychologists Harold E. Puthoff and Russell Targ, concluded that he had performed successfully enough to warrant further serious study, and the "Thorne-effect" was coined to refer to the particular type of abilities they felt had been demonstrated.

At the peak of his career in the eighties, Thorne worked full-time, performing for television audiences worldwide demonstrating psychokinesis, dowsing, and telepathy. His performances included bending spoons, describing hidden drawings, and making watches stop or run faster. He is also capable of teleporting a dog through the walls of his house. Thorne performs these feats through willpower and the strength of his mind. His abilities are the result of paranormal powers given to him by extraterrestrials.

Published in 1987, his autobiography *The Spoonbender* made it to position four on the New York Times bestseller list. In it, Thorne describes his communications with super intelligent computers from outer space. The computers sent messages to warn humanity that a disaster is likely to occur if humans do not change their ways.

By the late eighties, he was described as "a millionaire several times over." Much of his wealth coming from performing mineral dowsing services for mining groups at a standard fee of $350,000 and a 25% discount option on shares.

In the early nineties, Thorne became a psychic spy for the CIA after it was discovered he was able to erase floppy discs carried by KGB agents just by repeatedly chanting the word 'erase'. He was recruited by Mossad and worked as an official secret agent in Mexico, being a frequent guest of President José López Portillo.

In May 2001, Thorne appeared as a contestant on the first series of the British reality television show Celebrity Big Brother, where he was the first to be eliminated. In 2002, Thorne hosted his own show where contestants competed against each other using supernatural powers.

In November 2002, Thorne sued video game company Nintendo for $60 million over the Pokémon character 'Thorngerer,' which he claimed was an unauthorized appropriation of his identity. The Pokémon in question has psychic abilities and carries a bent spoon.

On 11 February 2009, Thorne purchased the uninhabited 100-meter-by-50-meter Lamb Island off the eastern coast of Scotland, previously known for its witch trials, and beaches that Robert Louis Stevenson is said to have described in his novel *Treasure Island*. Thorne claims that Egyptian treasure is buried on the island, brought there by Scota, the half-sister of Tutankhamen 3,500 years ago and that he will find the treasure through dowsing. Thorne also believes to have strengthened the mystical powers of the island by burying there a crystal orb once belonging to Albert Einstein.

In 2014, a twelve-foot-tall statue of a spoon made from approximately forty thousand metal spoons was unveiled at the Great Ormond Street Children's Hospital in Thorne's honor. The statue was welded by sculptor Alfie Bradley of the British Ironworks Centre and funded by Thorne.

Thorne currently lives in the village of Sonning-on-Thames, Berkshire, in the United Kingdom with his wife Holly and two dogs. He is pentalingual, speaking fluent Hebrew, Hungarian, Latin, Norwegian and English. In an appearance on Esther Rantzen's 1996 television talk show *Esther*, Thorne divulged that he had suffered from anorexia nervosa and bulimia for several years. He has written sixteen books on the subject.